Endorsements

This is not a martial arts book, but a metaphor that takes you on a journey to becoming a mature maker of disciples. Throughout history, whether it was God sending judges to His people to help restore them out of decades of rebellion, or a sports team hiring a new GM to restore them to former glory, the running theme has always been, "We have to get back to the foundations and basics." The prophet Jeremiah tells us, "Thus says the Lord: "Stand by the roads, and look, and ask for the ancient paths, where the good way is; and walk in it, and find rest for your souls..." (Jer. 6:16 ESV). This is an underpinning to the very foundational thing that Jesus has commissioned all of us to do—MAKE DISCIPLES, THAT CAN MAKE DISCIPLES, THAT CAN MAKE DISCIPLES!

Dr. David Jeremiah

Senior Pastor of Shadow Mountain Community Church
Founder of Turning Point Radio and Television Ministries
Bestselling author

I have had the privilege of walking with Gino Mingo for almost three decades. Throughout all these years, he has consistently made extraordinary disciples in all avenues of life. His life and ministry powerfully embody the command of Jesus in Matthew 28:19 to go into every nation and make disciples.

Jim Laffoon

Every Nation Churches and Co-Founder of Unite714

Gino Mingo is a serious disciple-maker. We've been friends for over 30 years and I've watched his relentless pursuit to honor Christ by reaching out to people from every nation with the message of the Gospel. *Black Belt Discipleship* records Gino's passion and practical experiences that will challenge and inspire you to devote your life to God's purposes in your generation.

Dr. Rice Broocks
Co-founder, Every Nation Churches
Bestselling author of *God's Not Dead*

As a former member of the military, I found discipline to be key to my success. I needed it to stay fit, maintain the skillsets I learned, follow, lead, and, most importantly, accomplish the missions set before me. Now, four years removed from the military and functioning as a spiritual leader in my community and home, I find discipline even more important, especially as it relates to spirituality. My good friend and brother in Christ, Gino Mingo, breaks down the essence of discipleship in a unique and concise way involving a martial arts belt system. He takes you on an amazing and suspense-filled journey where the lessons of discipleship and discipline are beat into you. What will come out is an ultimate spiritual warrior prepared for any foe that comes your way. I want to encourage you to show up to Gino's Dojo through *Black Belt Discipleship*; you won't regret the visit.

Remi Adeleke
Writer, Producer, and Former Navy Seal

Gratitude. I imagine this will be your overwhelming response to Gino Mingo's masterful book, *Black Belt Discipleship*. Gratitude to the Father, for saving us and calling us into a life well-lived. Gratitude to yourself, for taking the steps to move closer to the One who gave you breath. And gratitude to the author, for laying down a path to follow.

Once I started reading this guide to discipleship, I was captured. First, it envisions and equips you to live a life "transformed by intimacy," by being found daily in God's presence. Then it offers a roadmap for your daily walk and the tools to persevere through shortcomings and challenges as you move ever closer to the Author and Perfecter of your faith. Remember, it is not just a race to finish, but a journey through which to grow.

Ultimately, you move from being a disciple to a disciple-maker; one who can look to others and, like Paul, say "follow me as I follow Christ." One who, like Timothy, can entrust the Gospel to the faithful whom God develops into the able.

I've known Gino for nearly four decades. I stood next to him when he married his bride and I've watched him personally be transformed from one submitting to spiritual authority to one who leads others through those same steps. It's time for you to earn your belt!

AC Green
NBA Pro Athlete

Using examples from the Bible, the world of sports, and popular culture, Gino Mingo delivers a powerfully engaging book about the importance of authenticity and mastery in our walk with God and our ability to attract and mentor new followers of Jesus Christ. Mingo's accessible writing and deep scriptural knowledge make *Black Belt Discipleship* a must-read book for teachers and followers of the Christian faith.

Dr. Maya Rockeymoore Cummings
President & CEO, Global Policy Solutions

The word Christian is only mentioned three times in the Bible. The word disciple is mentioned more than 250 times! The law of repetition tells us that the more something is repeated the greater of importance it is. Let's be clear, Jesus never called his companions "Christians." He called them disciples.

Gino Mingo's, *Black Belt Discipleship* (BBD) is not just a discipleship manual for those who seek to become committed disciples of Jesus Christ, but is a manual to make "disciple-makers" who will in-turn, do the same. Mingo reveals the "early Christians" were not only followers of "The Way" — as in "the way, the truth and the life" — but Christ instructed, his soon-to-be apostles, very much like a sensei runs a dojo: I do, you watch; you do, I correct, and repeat. This "way" of training, or transformation, is antithetical to our Western understanding of teaching; you talk, I take notes, ask questions, and take a quiz.

BBD walks you through the hands-on process of spiritual development which can only be done relationally, transforming a follower, (literally) one who follows or comes after another, into a disciple — one is disciplined in the teachings of another; especially one who then teaches others.

This process of a "disciple-maker making disciple-makers" truly matures the body of Christ and exponentially grows lasting and self-replicating fruit that remains. *Black Belt Discipleship* requires that you "discipline your body like an athlete" (1 Cor. 9:27, NLT). It demands that you must engage in "cross-training" everyday by "picking up your cross" to follow Him in his dojo. While it is easy to spot an athlete, soldier, or fighter by how they look, it should be just as easy to spot a disciple of Jesus Christ by how he or she lives their lives.

Unfortunately, this is not always the case. I believe the problem we have today is too many undisciplined "Christians" whom, upon witnessing how they live, you would never know they were believers-- hence they are poor witnesses. Ultimately, it is not the uncommitted masses of Christians who change the world, it is the disciplined, committed few. Welcome to the dojo of Christ!

Lakita Wright
Vice President, Urban Outreach Foundation

Black Belt Discipleship

Imparting the Nature of a Disciple-Maker

Gino Mingo

Black Belt Discipleship: Imparting the Nature of a Disciple-Maker
Published by Now Found Publishing, LLC
Southlake, Texas
NowFoundPublishing.com

Edited by Courtney Cohen
Cover design by Steven Cohen

Trade Paperback ISBN: 978-1-942362-23-4
eBook ISBN: 978-1-942362-24-1

Black Belt Discipleship is also available on Amazon Kindle, Barnes &
Noble Nook, Google Play Books, and Apple iBooks.

Disclaimer: The opinions and observations expressed herein do not
necessarily reflect those of Now Found Publishing, LLC.

All Scripture quotations, unless otherwise indicated are taken
from the Holy Bible, English Standard Version, copyright 2001, by
Crossway Bibles, a division of Good News Publishers.

Contents

Black Belt Descipleship

It is not the dissemination of information, but the impartation, inculcation, and implementation that produces a manifest expression of that "said" information that makes all the difference.

Gino Mingo

To Robert,
Glad to have met another brother in the Lord. I look forward to advancing the Kingdom with you!

Lk. 6:40

In Him,

Gino

Foreword

Black Belt Descipleship

Foreword

"10 In—10 Out!" is a saying I've used for years. It means that if you want to be great in the game of life, you must put forth a "10" effort. You must invest a far greater than average amount of time, energy, sacrifice, commitment, and focus in order to get where you ultimately want to go.

I've seen what it takes to make it to the top. As a coach and trainer in the sports performance arena, I've had the opportunity to work with a fair share of elite athletes including Olympic gold medalists, NFL MVP's, Super Bowl MVP's and champions, MLB All-stars and World Series MVP's, Heisman trophy winners, and MMA World Champions.

There can only be so many at the top. For every "champion" athlete there are an exponential number of others who don't make it. While their mind and mouth may say, "*Coach, Coach, I want to be great. I want to go to the next level. I want to do what it takes,*" their will, effort, and physical ability have a much larger determining factor as to whether they will achieve those desires.

The difficulties lie where the training begins. Requiring incredible commitment levels, early mornings, long sessions, no lights, no cameras, no glory, no fame, only lots of sweat, tons of grind. Day after day, week after week, sometimes even year after year passes until full potential is reached. If you want to maximize your talents and God-given potential, it's going to require an "all-in" mentality. A mentality of "10 in—10 Out!" Anything less than a *10 in* will yield exactly that out.

Meet Gino Mingo. I've known him for 15 years and he epitomizes what the "10 In-10 Out" motto stands for. He's a devout husband to Michelle, now for over 20 years, an amazing father of five daughters, a pastor, coach, friend, and most importantly, he is a disciple of Jesus.

Since I first met Gino, he has exemplified the character of a soldier for God. He leads Bible studies; he's planted churches; he's spoken at my gyms and at national conferences; he's held one-on-one counseling sessions; he's discipled people of all ages, races, beliefs; and he has faced and overcome all sorts of challenges and obstacles.

Gino Mingo is a disciple of God. How he walks, how he talks (and oh-boy can he talk!!!), and how he lives his life as a father, husband, preacher, brother, and friend represents the way I believe Jesus would walk amongst the earth with each of us.

For years, I've been encouraging Gino to write a book. He has as much biblical knowledge, acumen, and prophetic gifting as anyone I know. Gino's faith emanates in a way that helps me imagine how Jesus Himself would radiate love, compassion, empathy, care, commitment, and devotion.

In his book, *Black Belt Discipleship*, Gino explores the levels towards becoming a disciple for Jesus. Just as a martial arts student moves from white belt to black belt, Gino describes how we can not only improve our own relationship with Jesus, but how we can walk amongst our peers, colleagues, friends, and family and truly be a man or woman of God that disciples *all* people to be more Christ-like.

As a man of faith myself, I often feel compelled to be a *better* disciple for Jesus. While I feel like I operate daily at different levels, every now and then I will get to a moment that Gino would reference as a "black-belt" moment, one of those moments when I feel so close to God and so intimate with Jesus that I am truly working and walking out my life's purpose.

I don't know about you, but I want more of those moments. I want more "10 Outs" in my life and I realize it will take more "10 Ins" in my life. It will take even more continual effort, discipline, commitment, sacrifice, and practice.

That's why I love *Black Belt Discipleship*. This book equips us with the knowledge and wisdom necessary to deepen our walks with Jesus so that we can live more Christ-like and, ultimately, *disciple* more people. Just like there is a hierarchy in martial arts with ascending belt-colors and depth of relationship with the master, there is a deepening of relationship with Jesus in our lives as we spend increasing time with Him. While you don't need a hierarchy to accept Jesus as your Lord and Savior, it does take ongoing study, wisdom, and time to truly become a disciple.

My friends, enjoy this incredible book! The world needs it now more than ever before. Heck, you and I need it more than ever before. If we can become even more

Christ-like in our walk with Jesus and we can become even stronger disciples of God, just think about all the extraordinary impact we can create to expand God's kingdom.

"10-In—10 Out!"

Much love...and lots of black-belt discipleship.

Todd Durkin, MA, CSCS
Owner, Fitness Quest 10 & Todd Durkin Enterprises
2-Time Trainer of the Year;
Author & Speaker

Foreword

Dynamic
Warm-Up

Dynamic Warm-Up

At the end of each chapter you will be invited to partake in what are called "Cool Down Devotional Stretches." These cool down devotional stretches will help aid your spiritual and mental muscles in the recovery process as you make small changes in your daily discipleship journey. These consistent changes will lead to an ongoing and powerful transformation. As you engage in the cool down devotional stretches, set the book down, pause, *selah*, and ruminate. This is a valuable time for self-reflection to reveal where you currently are in this journey and where you might be headed. Embrace this investment in lifelong, biblical principles as you download and consistently apply them throughout your life.

Salvation accomplished through the Cross was the manifested love and sacrificial expression of God the Father and His Son, Jesus Christ. Discipleship was the genius of Jesus that led the professors and leaders of that present day seminary, the Sanhedrin counsel, to arrive at the conclusion that "...these men had BEEN WITH JESUS."[1] Then, twenty plus years later, because of this type of discipleship, it provoked the bombastic declaration that "...these men...have turned the world upside down..."[2]

These cool down devotional stretching moments should move us to want to find someone in our sphere of existence who has lived that way--someone to relationally

1 - Acts 4:13, ESV
2 - Acts 17:6, ESV

imitate, to glean from, to catch what is coming out of them spiritually. If we do not, then we could be in danger of not only missing out on something extremely vital to our walk with God, but we could also fail to reveal that WE HAVE BEEN WITH JESUS! I do not say this to sound harsh or judgmental, any more than a sensei in any dojo would push you to be the best you could possibly be. I say this for two reasons: 1) Because I love you with the love of Christ, and 2) Because I'm more concerned about your character than your comfort, and your destiny that produces a legacy more than your circumstantial happiness.

Simply put, I want you to BECOME what God created you to be and eventually DO what God intended you to! So, please, take a deep dive into your cool down devotional stretches and enjoy the benefits you will truly receive!

Having said that, my wife, Michelle, is going to start you off with a *Dynamic Warm-Up* below to get your spiritual muscles activated for this journey through *Black Belt Discipleship*.

What is Discipleship?

Before we can talk about discipleship, which we will do extensively in this book, we must define our terms.

First, we need to understand that there are levels of discipleship.

Jesus taught the masses. He spoke to congregations in synagogues, to crowds in cities, and to the multitudes out in the countryside. This first level of discipleship, **Public Discipleship**, is what we experience when we go to a church service or listen to a speaker online, etc. *Public Discipleship* can be very effective in that *many* people can be hearing the *same* message at one time, and there is a certain unity of mind and heart when a group of people are receiving the same ideas at one time—a shared experience. However, *Public Discipleship* is the weakest form of discipleship, because ultimately, as Gino emphatically asserts...

Discipleship Is Relationship.

With this truth in mind, we understand that the closer and more intimate the relationship we have with someone, the more we become like them and the greater the impact we have upon them. This reality is why it is so crucial to develop the habit of continually spending intentional time with Jesus. We refer to this relational transference of character and nature as impartation.

Impartation in relationships is inevitable. We don't have to work at it—it just happens by being around someone. For me personally, if I am around an angry person, I have to work very hard not to become angry myself. If I am with a person who has a lot of peace and wisdom, I am easily peaceful myself. As I spend more and more time around that gentle person, their gifts and strengths actually begin to take root in my soul and permeate my nature, and, even when I am not around them, I am still peaceful, not just for a little while, but more permanently. Conversely, if I am continually in a negative environment, it is extremely difficult for me not to internalize hostility.

Anyone who is a parent knows that this principle of relational transference is fundamentally true. We parents tend to naturally be concerned about who our child is hanging out with and whether that person is a good influence or not.

I'm reminded of the saying, "Show me your friends, and **I'll show you your future**," because...

Discipleship Is Relationship.

The second level of discipleship is **Personal Discipleship**. Jesus had many people who, after having had an encounter with Him, were forever changed. As good Jews, they continued to attend *Shabbat* (or Sabbath) services at the synagogue, but they also began to meet "house to house" to worship the Lord.[3]

Now we're entering into the world of small groups: Sunday school classes, Bible study groups, home groups, mid-week meetings, and so forth. These types of gatherings provide us with the opportunity for *peer* discipleship. Personal Discipleship serves to reinforce and to put into practice the truths and principles we have all been learning in the shared Public Discipleship space. This is an opportunity for us to build closer **relationships**. (Ah hah! There's that word again! Why? Because... discipleship is relationship! You're getting good at this.)

We are intentionally creating a space, which we *hope* is safe, to share our thoughts and struggles and to *do life* with other believers, usually on a weekly basis, but hopefully more often as friendships continue to grow

3 - Acts 2:46

over time. Ideally, a type of extended family, spiritual family, if you will, is created.

Sometimes people take building community a step further and live in discipleship houses or apartments together with other believers, because they know that "iron sharpens iron" and because they want accountability and intimacy...family.[4] That concept may seem odd to some, but I lived in a sorority house in college with about forty other women, and no one ever seems to think that's strange. I also lived in numerous discipleship houses and shared a condo or two with other believers until I got married at the age of thirty-three. It was challenging at times, but it was also so much fun. I learned so much from all of my roommates and got a front row seat to different cultures, ethnicities, and socio-economic backgrounds. We all rubbed off on each other and spurred one another on to follow Jesus as we prayed together, went to church together, listened to each other's problems and rejoiced in each other's victories. We also got frustrated when others didn't clean up after themselves or were grumpy or selfish, and sometimes we got into arguments, just like in a family. It was incredible! Those are some of the best times of my life and many of those people are still some of my most trusted friends, even though we don't live close to each other anymore.

Personal Discipleship is much stronger than Public Discipleship alone.

Perhaps this breakdown seems rather elementary to you; however, it is at this second level of *Personal*

4 - Pr. 27:17

Discipleship that most people stop in their discipleship journey.

Gino Mingo is endeavoring to inspire us to go on to the next level—*Private Discipleship*. This is the level where we learn to open up our lives to another individual who is further down the road than we are (a sensei, if you will) with whom we can be totally honest without fear of judgment; someone who doesn't have ulterior motives or agendas for how we can benefit them. (As you'll discover, however, truly great relationships are always mutually beneficial and bring richness and tremendous blessing into each person's life.)

I'm going to be honest with you. Finding a person like the one I've described is extremely difficult, perhaps impossible, and that is why, ultimately, we are always disciples of Jesus, not Pastor Bob or even "of Paul" or "of Apollos."[5] Our job as disciplers is to help people grow closer to Jesus. "Follow me as I follow Christ," but follow Christ, first and foremost.[6] You belong to Jesus, not me, or Pastor Bob, or whoever disciples you. Jesus is responsible for you. *He* is the "author and finisher of our faith."[7] Then, *you* are ultimately responsible for your own growth--"... work out your own salvation with fear and trembling."[8] A discipler is there to help you discover and uncover what is inside of you, to draw out your strengths and to help educate and strengthen you in your weaknesses, but you are responsible for your own decisions, your own heart and mind, and your own relationship with God through Jesus. Each believer possesses what we refer to in

5 - 1 Cor. 3:4
6 - 1 Cor. 11:1
7 - Heb. 12:2
8 - Phil. 2:12

theological terms as an "individual priesthood." "For there is one God, one mediator between God and men, the man Christ Jesus."[9] I can't overstate the value of having godly people in our lives, but we must understand that even the best people will let us down in small or even big ways, for "none are good,"[10] and "none are righteous,"[11] and "all...fall short of the glory of God."[12]

I have been attempting to disciple others since I surrendered my life to Jesus in 1989 as a college student, and I've made lots of mistakes, but I still keep working at it and strive to continue learning to love people better, because He has commanded me (and you) to "make disciples."[13]

Now, I am a parent. I have five kids, ages 15, 14, 12, 11, and 9. Let me tell you, there's a lot of pressure doing life with these precious and extremely challenging young people, and I am NOT a perfect parent...but what is my choice? To not parent them? That's not an option. I don't have a choice. I must muddle through and do my very best, trusting that "love covers over a multitude of sin."[14] I don't have to be flawless. I do have to love them "in Spirit and in truth."[15] I do have to lay down my life for them, and serve them, and put their needs before my own every single day. I do have to teach, train, and discipline them. I do have to be humble. I do have to learn to allow them to express themselves fully so I can then address

9 - 1 Tim. 2:5
10 - Rom. 3:12, Ps. 14:3
11 - Rom. 3:10, Ps. 53:1-3
12 - Rom. 3:23
13 - Mt. 28:19-20
14 - 1 Pet. 4:8
15 - Jn. 4:24

the attitudes of their hearts and minister God's truth to them. I do have to always be listening to the Holy Spirit to correct me and to lead me as to how to minister to them. I do have to "lean not on my own understanding."[16] I do have to act in the fear of the Lord, knowing that these children belong to God first, and to me and my husband second. They are ultimately His children and His disciples.

Private discipleship goes beyond the experience of a large community experience of a church service, etc. Private discipleship moves past the mere small group experience which is more of a social nature. Jesus compels us forward into intimacy.

"What a man [person] desires most is unfailing love [unconditional love]..."[17]

Private discipleship is where the rubber meets the road. This is where things get real. It's not talk, it's not merely quoting a scripture or giving or receiving advice. This is family, because...

DISCIPLESHIP IS RELATIONSHIP.

God's plan for discipleship has always been the nuclear family. *The* Father, God the Father, is the head of the family. The extended family serves to support the younger nuclear families. The church supports all the families and serves the community at large. As we strive to grow together in Christ, our entire neighborhoods and cities will be transformed. A strong community is made

16 - Pr. 3:5-6
17 - Pr. 19:22

up of strong families.

When Jesus walked the earth, he called people to Himself to be His disciples. There were twelve closest to Him, and there were also some women who followed Him and travelled from town to town with Him.[18] Then, there was a larger group of 72 that were very close to Him as well and that He sent out to do ministry.[19]

Private discipleship is when we move into the place of exercising our individual priesthood by taking purposeful steps to draw close to Jesus while simultaneously allowing someone access to our lives, because they have welcomed us into theirs, which is called friendship. I'm reminded of the old hymn, "*What a Friend we have in Jesus, all our griefs and sins to bear...*"[i]

God offers us His friendship. In this book *Black Belt Discipleship*, Gino Mingo is offering you his.

18 - Lk. 8:1-3
19 - Lk. 10:1-23

Preface

Preface

By the grace of God, I have had the pleasure and privilege of reaching various levels of achievement in a variety of fields. I have recorded two albums as a professional vocalist, had an acting role in a movie, and even had a short stint in professional football. I have become a husband whose wife says he's doing a better-than-average job, a father whose five girls (so far) think he's hung the moon, a minister of the gospel of Jesus Christ, and, lastly, an avid maker of disciples. These diverse endeavors all required an extended amount of time to achieve. There's not much like the measurement of time to let you know what is most important to you in your life.

As a child, one thing I spent time on was watching martial arts films. Like many boys in my childhood era, I grew up as a die-hard Bruce Lee fan. I mean, who wouldn't have? I was such a fan that later in my life I started taking Wing Chun, the very fighting style that Bruce Lee and his sensei, Ip Man, made famous. Unfortunately, I had to suspend my lessons to prioritize quality family time with my wife and five princesses. So, I cannot boast of knowing what it feels like to attain a black belt in Wing Chun—maybe one day. I could name all of his movies. I remember going to see the movie *Game of Death* immediately after getting baptized in 1978 with my oldest friend and play cousin, Herb Jefferson. I can still see Los Angeles Laker Kareem Abdul-Jabbar's huge footprint across the chest of Bruce Lee's bright yellow jumpsuit with black stripes going down the sides—epic!

One particular scene in *The Return of the Dragon* stands out to me. Bruce gets shipped off to Rome to stay with his uncle because he'd been hanging with the wrong crowd, fighting too much in China where he grew up. His uncle and cousins own a Chinese restaurant, and all of the employees practice karate during their lunch break in the alley out back. Bruce is an expert in Chinese kickboxing but had promised his mother that he would do no fighting while in Rome. Well, the plot quickly reveals that Bruce's uncle is getting squeezed by a local gangster for protection money. And if his uncle doesn't pay, "There's going to be big trouble!" (Imagine the horribly dubbed, thickly accented English, lips out of sync with the sound.)

Well, the uncle decides not to succumb to the mobster's demands. So, of course, the mobster sends his cronies to the restaurant to collect by way of force. Although workers try to defend the restaurant, they're amateur karate students at best. In the alley during the fight, Bruce desperately wants to get into the battle and even the playing field, but he keeps having flashbacks of his promise to his mother amid pleas for help by his co-workers. Then, all of a sudden, unprovoked, out of nowhere, one of the hoodlums jumps in front of Bruce, rips off the necklace that his mother gave him, and throws it to the ground. Finally, Bruce has an excuse to enter the fray.

Of course, Bruce starts kickin' butt and takin' names. All the while, the co-workers stand back in awe of the skill and expertise that Bruce displays. At one point during the melee, Bruce pulls out his favorite weapon of choice from the back of his belt, the nunchaku (affectionately known in America as nunchucks). He goes to work, a man among boys! Suddenly, someone knocks the nunchucks out of Bruce's hand and picks them up. At first glance, the thug looks as though he knows how to handle the nunchucks. But when he attempts to strike Bruce with the nunchucks, he ends up knocking himself out cold (definitely a moment of comic relief, to say the least)! At that moment, as a young boy, I began to recognize that having head knowledge of something and heart knowledge of something are two entirely different things. (If you don't believe me, ask the guy who knocked himself out with the nunchucks.)

An often-heard story depicts the birth of the black belt in the martial arts. A trainee's belt, which, traditionally, was never washed, became progressively dirtier with time (started white, became yellow with sweat, green with grass stains, and so on) and, finally, changed to black over the years. This explanation, however fanciful, carries with it a profound meaning too rich to ignore. Once we step out of myth and legend, the best source of information on the meanings of belt colors concerning rank is most certainly one's teacher. As I said earlier, I am no black belt in Wing Chun. (I probably couldn't keep my pants up with a white belt at this particular moment.) But when it comes to making disciples, my metaphorical disciple-maker's belt in the spirit realm reflects a vintage, very worn, dingy, deep black shade. It has been tested over a very long time.

I am convinced that Jesus had a specific outcome in mind when referring to the condition of a disciple, especially *His* disciples—fully trained. "A disciple is not above his teacher, but everyone when he is fully trained will be like his teacher."[1] As Christians, professing followers of Jesus, this must be our disposition when it comes to discipleship. It's the disposition of other vocations and careers. When I say fully trained, I'm not saying you have to acquire a doctorate in the subject. Instead, consider the military. When someone joins the military, no matter what branch, they all have to complete boot camp before being referred to as a soldier. As a matter of fact, they're called all sorts of things before they're ever called "soldier," such as "maggot," "idiot," "imbecile," and "sorry excuse for a human being." (Actually, I'm being quite polite instead of using the really *nice* words they use to describe the soldiers-to-be.) Nevertheless, each recruit becomes qualified as a soldier before branching off and choosing areas to specialize in. Becoming a disciple doesn't imply that you have to become an apostle, prophet, evangelist, pastor, or teacher. It doesn't mean you have to get your master's degree in healing, prophesying, miracles, tongues, etc. It simply means that you are being transformed into a qualified soldier in the army of the Lord.

The purpose of writing *Black Belt Discipleship* was to help people understand the essence, the true nature, of a disciple-maker and what it takes to become one. Will you give me permission to speak into your life as you read this book and challenge you to go deeper in your understanding of what a disciple of Jesus and a disciple-maker truly look like? I had the privilege of playing on the Colorado AAU basketball team at age 14 and represent Colorado against other chosen states in the national

1 - Lk. 6:40 (ESV)

tournament. My hindsight highlight was playing against Del Curry, father of one of the best NBA players in the world, Steph Curry of the Golden State Warriors. I have up-close and personal knowledge of how Steph Curry became the best shooter in the world. He got it from his daddy! His dad instilled in him discipline and a strong work ethic. One of my favorite monikers given to Steph by NBA analysts is "Stephortless!" Here's the irony, the nickname was given to him because he puts so much effort into his training, making him so fruitful in his craft, that when he plays the game, he makes it look *effortless*. What if we put the same type of training into becoming Jesus' disciples—not Bob's, Chuck's, or Steve's disciples, but Jesus' disciples? The Bible says that when we tap into fruitfulness, it glorifies God, "...and we so prove to be [Jesus'] disciples."[2]

I believe where we have often failed in the body of Christ when it comes to discipleship is in the area of training. Remember this: training involves failure, but the more you train, the less you fail. Training leads to mastery, but most people are too impatient for mastery—"Just give me the quick-fix pill please!" George Leonard, author of *Mastery: The Keys To Success And Long-Term Fulfillment*, said this about our society in regards to mastery, "Our current society works in many ways to lead us astray, but the path to mastery is always there, waiting for us."[ii] This is so true. Everything we see – from ads to infomercials –shouts at us, "Turn in here! I'll show you the quickest, easiest way to your destination!" But anytime you are shaping, forming, cultivating, inculcating, or imparting the nature of something into someone, cutting corners is not an option. You cannot and will not be or produce

2 - Jn. 15:8 (NASB)

something you are not. And that's a fact, Jack!

As we embark on this journey of imparting the nature of a disciple-maker, you'll notice that the majority of the chapter titles include a belt color. The idea to parallel the colors with chapters came from looking at the meanings of each color in a martial arts system and realizing that the belt color meanings correspond to the condition of discipleship in the body of Christ. The progression is as follows:

- **White Belt**: Represents a birth or beginning of a seed. The white belt is the beginning of life's cycle.

- **Yellow Belt**: Represents the first beam of sunlight which shines upon the seed, equipping it for new growth in the spring. A yellow belt student is given his first ray of knowledge, opening his mind with the help of his instructor.

- **Orange Belt**: Represents the growing power of the sun. The orange belt begins to feel his body and mind open up and develop.

- **Green Belt**: Represents the growth of the seed progressing into a plant. A green belt student learns to strengthen and refine his techniques.

- **Blue Belt**: Represents the sky as the plant continues to grow toward it. The blue belt student feeds on additional knowledge of the art for his body and mind to continue growing and developing.

- **Purple Belt**: Represents the changing sky of

dawn, as once again the student undergoes a new change and prepares for the transition to an advanced student. A purple belt begins to understand the meaning of the black belt.

- **Brown Belt**: Represents the ripening of the seed, a maturing and harvesting process. A brown belt is an advanced student whose techniques are maturing, and he is beginning to understand the fruits of his hard work as a beginner.

- **Red Belt**: Represents the heat of the sun as the plant continues growing toward it. As a red belt student acquires more detailed knowledge, just as the plant grows slowly toward the sun, so the red belt student learns to be more cautious with his knowledge and physical abilities. Red is a sign of danger, and the red belt is beginning to become dangerous with their knowledge and abilities.

- **Black Belt**: Represents the darkness beyond the sun. A black belt seeks new, more profound knowledge of the art. As he begins to teach others, he plants new seeds and helps them grow and mature. His students, many of whom will form deep roots into the art, blossom and grow through the ranks in a never-ending process of self-growth, knowledge, and enlightenment.

What I have noticed through nearly 30 years of ministry is that most of the church in America that I've encountered would fall into the range of white belt to blue belt. If you look over those colors again, you'll find that those colored belts are very myopic and egocentric. This belt range is centered around the individual and their personal growth and well-being. Now that's not a problem in the beginning because we're learning. The problem is that we're *staying* in that belt range, which doesn't do much in regards to healthy growth in the body of Christ. It actually causes stunted growth.

Now, when you arrive at the purple to black range, you start stepping into the fully-trained mindset of Jesus. This mindset is *other-centric* instead of *egocentric*, which produces the fruit—love and selflessness—Jesus wants us to impart to others. Until we get out of the white to blue range and into the purple to black range, we're going to remain somewhat anemic in our discipleship efforts. Make no mistake about it. You're not a black belt disciple-maker until your disciples are making disciples who are making disciples. Paul put it this way when talking to his disciple and son in the Lord, Timothy, "The things which you have heard from me in the presence of many witnesses, entrust these to faithful men who will be able to teach others also."[3] The process may seem long and overwhelming, but don't get nervous—just go getcha white belt! It's time to get after it and get it dirty!

3 - 2 Tim. 2:2

Preface

Introduction

Black Belt Descipleship

Introduction

It's Saturday morning in the early '70s, and *The Jetsons* cartoon plays on my television. Jane throws a pill into the futuristic microwave and—*voilà*—out pops a three-course meal! The signs were quite obvious then that the future was all about making things happen faster.

I have observed the American church over the past twenty-plus years. During that time, I have been connected in various capacities to three different church movements and six different churches, and I am currently in the midst of planting another one. The church does not appear to be much different from *The Jetsons* in its attempts to fulfill the Great Commission presented by Jesus thousands of years ago. But that wasn't Jesus' process. His process was the relational impartation of life. It involved walking with His disciples and doing life together—a covenant relationship. I can clearly remember preparing a message in a series on discipleship and hearing the Lord tell me to ask the congregation this question: "What are you going to say when I ask you if you've made any disciples during your time here on earth?"

As a church leader, I have found it somewhat disheartening when we (although probably subconsciously) attempt to improve upon Jesus' perfect model of discipleship. What do I mean? Jesus wasn't just perfect in the sense that He was simply mature and complete in what He did. No, He was also flawless in everything He did. And His model of discipleship has always been, and will always be, about the covenant process of imparting life—not didactically filling someone's head with information. We should be careful of thinking that we have modeled His example just because we have passed some of His information along.

Whether we realize it or not, we are always being taught something. Many say, "Life is a lesson in and of itself." But what I know to be true is this: It's who you are that gets imparted into another person, not just what you say. Jesus could have simply left us with the perfect life manual and made it the most theologically and doctrinally sound manuscript ever...He actually did. It's called the Bible! But even Jesus said in that Bible, "You search the scriptures because you think that in them you have eternal life; it is these that testify about Me; and you are unwilling to come to Me so that you may have life."[1] He wanted people to come to Him so that He could impart life into them. And when they read the scriptures through the foundation of an intimate relationship with Him, the scriptures would testify and confirm the undeniable fact of who Jesus was in their lives. But, instead, they settled for simply accumulating information from the scriptures and called that a relationship with Jesus. I wonder who is really willing today to take the time to emulate Jesus and invest at least three and a half years into a person to help them become like Jesus' disciples? As the old adage says, "More is caught than taught!" That is the impartation of life!

Why do we struggle to remember the three or four

1 - Jn. 5:39-40

points the pastor made on Sunday? I can't count the times I've heard someone say, "That message sure was good!" or "Pastor so-n-so was on fire today!" But when asked, "What were the points Pastor so-n-so made?" we look up into the sky and say, "Man, I'm having trouble remembering—but it sure was good!" The reason why this happens is that we've been trained, especially here in America, to learn mainly through a Greek didactic methodology. In other words, our main way of learning is by being lectured to and then, later, regurgitating it from memory simply to pass a test or get a certain grade in school.

God has created us to rise up to another level of living through challenges. Do I proclaim myself an expert at discipleship? It depends on your definition of discipleship and who is doing the asking. But as the saying goes, "It's not experience that makes the difference, but evaluated experience that makes all the difference."

I think it's time, as a whole, that we start evaluating our discipleship and the actual fruit being produced. The Bible clearly says, "For it is time for judgment to begin at the household of God..."[2] In other words, as the ones who carry the standards of God, we should be the ones who hold our noses to that standard. It's our responsibility first, not society's. And for those who pastor large churches, mega-churches, oversee multiple churches, movements, etc., you have certainly accomplished something I have not in regards to the size of your churches. Without question, you have an incredible platform from which to advance the kingdom. But there could still be some calibrating that needs to take place in the area of disciple-making. What pastor worth his salt hasn't at some point

2 - 1 Pet. 4:17a

desired to bolster the quality of what's being produced in his work—even if that work is already good?

I recognize that, for larger churches, engaging in some of the concepts I endeavor to present could cause frustration. It could mean having to downshift to neutral while trying to figure out how to apply these principles in your setting. Slowing the machine down is no easy task. But what should be comforting to everyone is that nothing is impossible with God. It just means hard work ahead—hard work empowered by His grace to turn the ship around or to plot a new course.

Another observation I've made regarding the American church is the obsession of crafting impeccable Sunday morning productions, empowered by sterling silver polished light shows to be attractive or relevant. Please don't get me wrong, there certainly needs to be ample time given to crafting sermons and honing communication skills. No one wants to get stuck listening to someone who can't string coherent sentences together which fail to produce clearly understood thoughts and concepts regarding God. But sometimes more attention is given to that than to discipling the body so that it can lead and disciple the lost into the family of God. And many times we get caught in that trap because we want to be attractive and draw in as many people as we can—and rightly so! But remember, whatever you use to "get 'em" is what you will have to use to "keep 'em". So we might want to use what Jesus used—His Word mixed with power. We'll come back to this later. Onward we go!

Let's be clear. At the judgment seat of Christ, we are not going to be asked, "Did the lights switch at the right time when the music changed?" or "Did the slides come up at the right time when I made my third point?" However, we might be asked, "Did you make any disciples while here on Earth?"

Again, please don't misunderstand me. I, too, am all for excellence on a Sunday morning. But I find that the excellent shows we have been putting on have also spoiled the congregation for the wrong things at times. Spiritual pundits have observed that people are getting disillusioned with church and are leaving what they call "that church thang." We can't fall into the human trap of being overly concerned about appearance. The Scriptures say, "...For the Lord sees not as man sees: man looks on the outward appearance, but the Lord looks on the heart."[3] We need a paradigm shift in our thinking. Although it's okay to look good, it's not about the appearance we have, but the presence we carry.

What we truly carry within us is determined by our nature. It is about what people recognize at a deeper level in our lives. Wasn't that Jesus' model? The Word tells us that "...He had no form or majesty that we should look at him, and no beauty that we should desire him."[4] He wasn't going to make the cut for People Magazine's "Most Beautiful" or grace the cover as the sexiest man alive. What He carried was neither on the surface nor a persona He was putting on. What He carried was who He was, is, and will always be. He lived a façade-free life.

So what was it then? Could it have been His presence they encountered? His presence as a disciple of

3 - 1 Sam. 16:7b (ESV)
4 - Isa. 53:2b

our Heavenly Father? It was made clear in Isaiah when it was prophetically said of Jesus, "The Lord God has given Me the tongue of disciples, that I may know how to sustain the weary one with a word. He awakens Me morning by morning, He awakens My ear to listen *as a disciple* [emphasis added]."[5] And boy, did He ever sustain them with a word—He is still sustaining people today with His Word. How they marveled at His presence and authority when He spoke! How they were enamored with His wisdom and power! The very nature that emanated from Him was disarming, to say the least. He was and is, not only Lord, Savior, King, Priest, Prophet, Healer, Shepherd, big brother, and friend, but He was and is also a disciple according to Isaiah. I believe it's now time to unspoil the congregation and get back to the Great Commission: making disciples of all ethnicities—not a watered-down version, but Jesus' model of making authentic disciple-makers!

Before we can move forward, we must first understand what the true nature of a legitimate disciple-maker of Jesus Christ is. Generally speaking, everyone is making disciples in different genres of society (i.e. the business world, the martial arts, sports, other religions, etc.), but for those of us who claim His name and are members of His family, are we truly making what Jesus Christ would call disciples?

As we set out on this journey, it is paramount to understand the framework for what I'm trying to convey by the phrase "imparting the nature of a disciple-maker." The purpose of imparting something is to give a deeper understanding, not simply to disseminate a surface

5 - Isa. 50:4

level knowledge. The goal is to make something become second nature. Second nature is when a habit or skill has been acquired and deeply ingrained. We brush our teeth without thinking about the process because the repetitive action has caused it to become ingrained in us.

I believe that Jesus' desire for us is that disciple-making would not become a mindless habit like brushing our teeth or putting on our clothes, but, rather, a thoughtful, deeply ingrained skill and habit that would impart the essence of Jesus to others as we walk with Him. No one is born a disciple of Christ, just like no one is born a concert pianist. When my dad bought me my first football helmet at age seven, that didn't make me a football player. Quite the contrary, it was the monotonous, continual coaching (impartation), practicing, and training over twenty years that allowed me to become a football player and eventually reach the NFL. Whether you're trying to become a football player, Navy SEAL, Jedi Master, or a black belt disciple-maker, there's no getting around the fact that you will need to have the nature of what you want to become imparted into to you.

Chapter 1

The Nature of a Disciple

Chapter 1: The Nature of a Disciple

During a very interesting conversation with a Navy SEAL instructor friend of mine about becoming a Navy SEAL, I asked, "What is your main purpose in BUD/S (Basic Underwater Demolition/Seal) training?" His reply was, "To get them to quit!" I laughed because of the matter-of-fact tone, but within that little statement was a hidden revelation. Whether you are becoming a part of an elite Navy SEAL team or becoming a part of Jesus' team of disciple-makers, the first and most important thing is to settle the issue and decide to become one. You cannot and will not be or produce something you are not!

Before we focus on the *process* of becoming a black belt disciple-maker, we should focus on the *purpose* of becoming one. The process carries very little punch until the purpose has been settled. Jesus said, "Go therefore and make disciples of all the nations..."[1] The purpose of being a disciple is to be a whole-hearted follower of Jesus Christ who is trained well enough to make other disciples. But the evidence of this is not that clear or plentiful today in the body of Christ.

When you read about the seven sons of Sceva—"I adjure you by Jesus whom Paul preaches!..."[2] —you find that those gentlemen got ahold of the process of

1 - Mt. 28:19
2 - Acts 19:13-17

deliverance. But what they did not have within themselves was the understanding of deliverance that Jesus and Paul had. What existed in the nature of Jesus and Paul was the purpose of deliverance and their legitimate relationship with the Heavenly Father. So, when someone sets out on the journey to become a disciple-maker, to be truly effective, they need to have the nature and essence of a disciple within them because you cannot and will not be or produce something you are not! This was implied when Jesus, being one Himself, said to go make disciples. And you're not a black belt disciple-maker until your disciples are making disciples who are making disciples!

This "discipleship thing" is first and foremost about *being* (essence) before *doing* (task). It's no secret how consumeristic we are here in America, concentrating our focus on the systems to produce a plethora of products and services as fast as possible, many times sacrificing value or the essence we were originally after. In the case of discipleship, we sometimes forego that which Jesus truly wanted from us—to become like Him, pleasing to the Father while making disciples.

Theologians tell us Jesus walked with His disciples approximately eighteen months before He sent them out on any assignment. I'm not saying we have to wait eighteen months before encouraging our disciples to go do something. But it does seem to take time to develop the right character and understanding necessary to become a mature disciple. This is definitely food for thought.

Years ago, I heard the story of a talented young basketball player I had enjoyed watching play in college who later made it to the NBA. He was from Chicago and played collegiate basketball in the state of Illinois. And, of course, his favorite player was Michael Jordan, who played for the Chicago Bulls. He, like many others at that time, wanted to "be like Mike." So when he made it to the NBA, he embarked on a journey to find out all of Michael Jordan's routines involving basketball. He discovered that Michael Jordan wore his University of North Carolina blue practice shorts from his college days under his NBA uniform while playing in the games. He also found out what pre-game meals Jordan ate, what workout regimens he used to stay in shape, as well as other various Jordan-esque rituals. The "faux-tégé" decided to wear his own alma mater's shorts under his pro team's uniform, eat the same pre-game meals, and follow Michael's workout regimens. But, what he didn't do was get down to the nitty-gritty of what Michael Jordan did to become, arguably, the greatest basketball player of any era.

Now on the flip side, there was another basketball player who wanted to "be like Mike" or better than Mike but refrained from copying Jordan's uniform or pre-game meal rituals. He set out to glean all he could from Michael Jordan regarding the game of basketball and diligently applied it to his skill set during his illustrious career. And, to this day, Kobe Bean Bryant (R.I.P. Mamba), more than any other NBA player, draws the most comparisons to the great Michael Jeffrey Jordan—and rightly so! Instead of simply adopting techniques and looking or acting like Mike, Kobe took on his attitude of determination, his work ethic, attached it to his already tenaciously competitive nature, and became the best at his position since Mike.

Kobe never would have been Michael Jordan, and we will never be Jesus, but we can draw comparisons to

Him if we diligently apply, through the Holy Spirit, all that Jesus has left us in His Word to become His disciples and top-notch disciple-makers. Now you may be saying to yourself, "I'm not sure I signed up to be a spiritual Michael Jordan or Kobe Bryant. I'm just glad I'm not going to be a crispy critter when it's all said and done and the end comes." But Jesus did say, "The disciple is not above his teacher, but everyone when fully trained, will be like his teacher."[3]

So what can we ascertain from this scripture? Before answering this question, please take a moment and try to think like Jesus as a Middle Easterner and not like a Westerner, who is inclined to think didactically. The word *train* implies much more than simply sitting before a purveyor of information. It implies teaching repetitively and persistently, causing rumination, and even failure, which ultimately leads to success. Failure played a major role as I learned how to become a professional football player as well as most of the other things I have achieved in life. We are not called to just be a part of God's family, simply family members. No, we are called to be disciple-makers!

Jesus' bidding, "Come, follow Me!" and use of the phrase "Be My disciple" are synonymous. There is not a second or third option available. I have a family of seven. Six of us could be disciples in our household, and one could be missing the mark. That doesn't mean the one missing the mark is not a part of our family—it just means the one is not a disciple. Jesus shed some light on this subject when dealing with Nicodemus during their late-night rendezvous:

3 - Lk. 6:40 (ESV)

Now there was a man of the Pharisees, named Nicodemus, a ruler of the Jews; this man came to Jesus by night and said to Him, "Rabbi, we know that You have come from God as a teacher; for no one can do these signs that You do unless God is with him." Jesus answered and said to him, "Truly, truly, I say to you, unless one is born again he cannot see the kingdom of God." Nicodemus said to Him, "How can a man be born when he is old? He cannot enter a second time into his mother's womb and be born, can he?" Jesus answered, "Truly, truly, I say to you, unless one is born of water and the Spirit he cannot enter into the kingdom of God. That which is born of the flesh is flesh, and that which is born of the Spirit is spirit. Do not be amazed that I said to you, 'You must be born again.'" [4]

Nicodemus was hung up on the *being born again* imagery, and Jesus was focusing on the *kingdom of God* reality. Being born again simply qualifies you to be able to see and enter into the kingdom of God. Once that happens, the next essential step is being trained to function in that spiritual kingdom because, again, you cannot and will not be or produce something you are not! Being trained is of eminent importance. And training should always start at the beginning.

The beginning of anything starts with first *settling the issue* in one's heart. When it comes to salvation, being a disciple, or walking in your calling, settling the issue always involves the immutable principle of the lordship

4 - Jn. 3:1-7

of Jesus. Whether we are talking about Elisha following Elijah, Peter walking with Jesus, or you becoming a disciple, it's ultimately about lordship:

> *Peter, turning around, saw the disciple whom Jesus loved following them; the one who also had leaned back on His bosom at the supper and said, "Lord, who is the one who betrays You?" So Peter seeing him said to Jesus, "Lord, and what about this man?" Jesus said to him, "If I want him to remain until I come, what is that to you? You follow Me [emphasis added]!"*[5]

That is lordship. Another way to say it could have been, "What's that to you? You be and do what I have called you to!" It seems like Peter was being challenged to *settle the issue* all over again.

Cool Down Devotional Stretches:

I am an avid basketball lover! I have had the pleasure of playing with and against All-Stars and Hall of Famers such as Gary Payton, Terrell Brandon, AC Green, Del Curry, Dave Jamerson, Brent Barry, and others. It was always fun to watch guys who thought of themselves as "basketball players" play in a pick-up game against actual NBA players. When these guys walked off the court, you could tell by their disposition that their thinking had changed a bit, that they no longer thought of themselves as "basketball players," but thought more like this, "I just play basketball (LOL)." Proverbs says, "For AS he thinks within himself, so he IS."[6] It's time to take the magnifying

5 - Jn. 21:20-22
6 - Pr. 23:7

glass and place it over your heart. You only live out what is in your heart (nature), not what's in your head.

What areas of your walk with God resemble the basketball analogy? What can you do to change the "way" you think that could lead you to become like the disciples in the Bible and eventual disciple-makers?

Chapter 2

Lordship

Chapter 2 - White Belt: Lordship

When the Father decided that it was time for the Son to shed His state of anonymity, Jesus quickly encountered some of His future disciples, who were at the time disciples of John the Baptist. And rightly so, since John was the forerunner to Jesus. These men followed John because he preached things of God that resonated in their hearts and exposed the religious hypocrisy prevalent in their time. Then, one day, along came this Jesus with a message that took things to a whole 'nother level.

Imagine you are Peter. You keep hearing about this Man your brother, Andrew, introduced you to and the ruckus He's been stirring up, especially among the religious people. Also, John the Baptist, the guy Andrew and your fishing partner, John, were following, starts telling everyone that Jesus is the one you really ought to be following. Then, one morning after you have been working hard throughout the night trying to catch fish, you see this large crowd forming near the seashore where you keep your fishing boat. You say to yourself, "Huh, it's Him again?" All the people are waiting to hear from Jesus whom John the Baptist keeps referring to as "the Coming One."

Well, before you know it, this Jesus character just steps into your boat and asks you to push out a little ways from the shore to create some space because the crowd that was pressing in on Him too much. Now, mind you, we are talking about Peter here. So, if you don't mind, I'm going to take a little creative license here and tell you what I imagine Peter was probably thinking. "Are you kidding me! Man, I've been working all night long, and I'm dead-dog-tired. I can't say no 'cuz now all these people are looking at us. And, if that ain't enough, now I gotta sit here in this boat as His captive audience until He gets done!" But little did Peter know that this moment in time was orchestrated mainly for him and his fishing companions, nor did Peter realize that a life-changing blessing was just around the corner.

Finally, Jesus gets done droppin' knowledge or, should I say, droppin' life on the crowd, and then He proceeds to tell Peter to push out into the deep water and go fishing! Back into Peter's mind we go: "Unbelievable! Now, I know you're good at what you do, but fishing's my thing! But since John the Baptist thinks so highly of you, I'm gonna give you the benefit of the doubt. Master, we worked hard all night and caught nothing, but I will do as you say and let down the nets."

Now imagine this, you're extremely tired, you have people that depend on your fishing business, and you're discouraged because you didn't catch any fish the night before. Furthermore, Jesus inconveniences you and asks you to do something that makes absolutely no sense. But you go along with it because you don't want to look bad in front of all the people who just spent an hour or two listening to all the things He had to say. Then, all of a sudden, the most amazing thing happens to you. Your fishing net fills up to the point where it starts to rip. You have to call your friends over to help you so you don't lose your miracle catch—a catch so large that both boats

White Belt: Lordship

begin to sink. This was probably the most significant moment yet in Peter and his friends' lives. It brought them face-to-face with the awesomeness of God! It produced in Peter and his friends the sobering reality of how unholy they were and how holy Jesus is. So much so, that they fell at Jesus' feet, and Peter asked Jesus to leave his presence. That's quite a life-altering moment.

But, what I believe was just as significant that I think people tend to gloss over was the magnitude of their response. Jesus told them, "...Do not be afraid; from now on you will be catching men,"[1] and, "I will make you fishers of men."[2] The Bible continues to say that when they got to shore they left everything and followed Him. Have we truly understood the revelation that caused such a radical transformation in them? Was it just a general revelation that God is awesome, all-powerful, and all-knowing? Or was it something on a deeper, more personal level? I say emphatically, "Yes!" to the latter. The ability of these fishermen to walk away from the greatest fishing expedition they had ever experienced was caused by a deeper revelation. God calls us beyond our personal needs into our destiny to become his disciples and disciple-makers.

This revelation must be imparted and inculcated into our hearts so that it becomes a part of our very nature through the constant relationship with Jesus and His other disciples. Jesus reminded His disciples of this:

They began to discuss with one another the fact that they had no bread. And Jesus, aware of

1 - Lk. 5:10b
2 - Mt. 4:19

69

this, said to them, "Why do you discuss the fact that you have no bread? Do you not yet see or understand? Do you have a hardened heart? Having eyes, do you not see? And having ears, do you not hear? And do you not remember, when I broke the five loaves for the five thousand, how many baskets full of broken pieces you picked up?" They said to Him, "Twelve." "When I broke the seven for the four thousand, how many large baskets full of broken pieces did you pick up?" And they said to Him, "Seven." And He was saying to them, "Do you not yet understand?"[3]

Here is another way of putting it: "Don't you get it, yet? I am your provision. I will meet your needs. I have called you beyond your needs into your destiny. Wake up!" Once that happens, the revelation that our vocation is simply the vehicle by which we fulfill the call of God on our lives to be disciple-makers is just moments away.

Something major had to have happened in their hearts during that remarkable moment to move them to leave everything—boats, nets, fish, their livelihood—behind. In their hearts, they did what I call "settling the issue." It involves the most preeminent concept of your walk with Jesus—lordship! This is the issue that must be settled up front to become a true disciple. Actually, it is *the* issue in *every* area of your life that must be settled. Who is sitting on the throne of your heart? You or Jesus? Money or Jesus? Career or Jesus? Relationships or Jesus? Family or Jesus? This issue of lordship is something that can be settled overnight, but not walked out overnight. On the contrary, it must be walked out over every night for the

3 - Mk. 8:16-21

rest of your life! When you read the Bible, start paying closer attention to Jesus' interactions with people. You will see that He is constantly moving them to a place of needing to settle the issue.

Could a loving God, this Jesus, have rigid and severe demands or requirements of us? Actually, yes! Just as any loving parent would have, so our loving God does. The New American Standard Bible version includes a section title over Luke 9:57-62 that reads, "Exacting Discipleship." Exacting means to be severe in demands on someone's effort, precision, and other resources. It seems that the body of Christ has gotten so wrapped up in the concept of "freedom in Christ" that it overlooks the fact that Jesus had some highly demanding requirements of His disciples. It is my opinion that the majority of believers in America could not call themselves disciples because they have not graduated from the white belt level in their walk with God.

Cool Down Devotional Stretches:

I spent about 15 years after my salvation experience disregarding lordship, thinking that my salvation was really just about having my fire insurance card so I could get into heaven. It was not until I had a staggering moment reading Jesus' words, "*Do not MARVEL that I said you, 'You must be born again.'*" (Jn. 3:7 ESV) As amazing as salvation is, here Jesus is saying do not be astonished at "being born again!" Instead, understand that "being born again" qualifies you to see and enter into the Kingdom of God! A kingdom has a king, and a king has an agenda, a system, a way that their subjects conduct themselves and adhere to the king's agenda. Our King's agenda is accomplished through lordship, which is a foundational block towards becoming His disciple.

Alright, time to hit the pause button--drop the book and search your heart to listen to where your resonators are humming. What are the areas of your life that have been myopic and focused on the benefits of salvation as opposed to submitting to lordship and God's desire for you to become His disciple? What things in your life have been vying for lordship, causing you to be unconsciously insubordinate?

White Belt: Lordship

Chapter 3

Self-Denial

Black Belt Descipleship

Chapter 3 - Yellow Belt: Self-Denial

Imagine that you are Jesus and talk of how you fed five thousand men, plus women and children, has spread throughout the region. While you are traveling along the road someone yells out to you, "I'll follow you wherever you go!" Now, most of us would probably respond with a resounding "Hallelujah! Grab your tunic, and let's boogie!" But no, not Jesus. It wasn't enough for Him to have people just simply follow Him. He wanted to make sure that their motives were lined up with God's motives.

I imagine the rest of His disciples were thinking, "Great, the more the merrier!" But Jesus quickly goes into a sobering explanation of what it is like to follow Him: "And Jesus said to him, 'The foxes have holes and the birds of the air have nests, but the Son of Man has nowhere to lay His head.'"[1] In other words, Jesus is saying:

> *Look, I perceive your motives are a little off. You want to follow me because you've heard of or seen how I've provided for people. You've seen the magic shows I've put on at times—but that ain't it folks! Sink your teeth into this—this ain't no easy trek. You had better settle the issue of lordship or you ain't gonna cut it! It is of the utmost importance that*

1 - Lk. 9:58 [parapharase mine]

you learn how to deny yourself! Furthermore, I'm
looking to lay my head, my authority, on those who
are mature enough to handle it. Is that you?

If you will allow me to pull the prophetic curtain back a little, Isaiah the prophet tells us, "For a child will be born to us, a son will be given to us; and the government will rest on His shoulders..."[2] Government often means *headship*. And for those who follow Christ, it is not uncommon for them to be referred to as "The Body of Christ." Therefore, metaphorically speaking as well as spiritually speaking, Jesus, being the head of the body, wants to rest His "Head" (His government) upon us, His body! But government doesn't just mean *dominion* or *rule*; it is *the steersman's art*, the art of guiding aright the vessel of church or state.[iii] It is integral influence at its best.

So in Jesus' eyes, how does that happen? It happens when our intimacy deepens because our pursuit of Him increases. It happens when we understand how intensely He desires us to be like His personal, trained, learned, practiced ones — His expert pupils and whole-hearted followers. Or, as I like to say, "His Navy Seal, Jedi-Master, Black Belt Disciple-Maker!" When this heart disposition is developed within us, it results in a dissatisfaction with "just" being saved. I personally believe that Jesus struggles with the casual inquirer because He did not casually die on the cross for us! Jesus is not interested in us being disciples of a religion, worldview, ideology, or unfounded presupposition. No, Jesus is interested in us being relationally consumed by Him! So, in essence, Jesus is trying to find those who will humble themselves in such a way that He can give them the

2 - Isa. 9:6

kind of authority to guide people into the things of His kingdom. He is looking to lay His *head*, His *government*, on people who embody that character. For Him to do that, the issue of lordship and denying one's self has to be settled and sewn into the very fabric of our nature, or we will never graduate from the yellow belt level!

Being human we are, by nature, selfish and we can feel entitled at times—actually, most of the time. We have all experienced at some level the sensation of pressure when someone was being exacting in our lives. It is exacting when a coach or someone in a place of authority asks us to give up or sacrifice something. Especially when, more times than not, we want to have our cake and eat it too. It is our cake, right? But, I suppose, Jesus has a right to compel us to follow Him into a discipleship relationship since He sacrificed His life to give all of us the opportunity of eternal life.

I can hear some of those I have pastored and discipled over the years say, "But isn't sacrifice and denying yourself the same thing?" No, not completely. You can sacrifice something and still do so selfishly; but you cannot move in selflessness, deny your *self*, and be selfish. By definition, selflessness means thinking of yourself secondarily, not primarily. Again, Jesus said, "If anyone wishes to come after me, he must deny himself..."[3] The apostle Paul put it this way:

> *Do nothing from selfishness or empty conceit,*
> *but with humility of mind regard one another*
> *as more important than yourselves; do not*

3 - Mk. 8:34

merely look out for your own personal interests, but also for the interests of others. Have this attitude in yourselves which was also in Christ Jesus, who, although He existed in the form of God, did not regard equality with God a thing to be grasped, but emptied Himself, taking the form of a bond-servant, and being made in the likeness of men. Being found in appearance as a man, He humbled Himself by becoming obedient to the point of death, even death on a cross. For this reason also, God highly exalted Him, and bestowed on Him the name which is above every name, so that at the name of Jesus EVERY KNEE WILL BOW, of those who are in heaven and on earth and under the earth, and that every tongue will confess that Jesus Christ is Lord, to the glory of God the Father.[4]

The goal of discipleship is the impartation of life, not classroom or book-smart teaching. "A pupil is not above his teacher; but everyone, after he has been *fully trained* [not just downloaded with information—emphasis mine], will be like his teacher."[5] Do you know how many pupils in the American education system leave the classroom without ever becoming like their teacher? (In some cases, that may be a good thing.) However, we see through Jesus' Jewish mindset that true impartation doesn't even really start in the training process until pupils decide to deny themselves.

When leaders in the church, those called to equip the body of Christ, fail to drive home the importance of

4 - Phil. 2:3-11
5 - Lk. 6:40

denying oneself in the discipleship process, we subject people to major challenges when they try to disciple others. If this does happen, there will be three major obstacles to overcome:

Fear of Being Exposed: You have to first become a disciple before you can make legitimate disciples. You will never feel adequate or effective in your task until you can answer *yes* to this question: "Do you believe you can impart the life and ways of Jesus Christ into someone else?" You will never act in a consistent manner contrary to your nature! That is why it is about the impartation of the nature of a disciple and not about the dissemination of information. You can only truly give what you possess. If you try to consistently give something spiritual that you do not possess, it will be exposed very quickly.

Fear of Responsibility: We cannot help but feel the pressure that comes with the reality of someone following or trusting us to convey the life of Christ. Therefore, the possibility of failure looms over us like a dark storm cloud. But the Apostle Paul said, "Be imitators of me, just as I also am of Christ."[6] So then, if we are being true disciples, walking in faith (relying upon Him), we should understand that He has set us up to "overwhelmingly conquer through Him who loved us,"[7] and not to fail. Don't get me wrong, I am not pushing flawlessness! Though failures are a part of the journey, many times they are also stepping stones to our success! We are a work in progress until we leave this earth. But we're also on a journey where God is encouraging us as His body to grow up into the mature stature of Christ!

6 - 1 Cor. 11:1
7 - Rom. 8:37

The simple truth is that God would never call us to do something that He would not empower us to accomplish.

Selfishness: I believe this is self-explanatory. If we are being selfish and not getting outside of ourselves for the sake of others, then we are moving in an attitude that is antithetical to the character of Jesus. Therefore, it is a fallacy to say you are being like Him if your attitude, your heart disposition, is the exact opposite.

The only way to overcome these hang-ups is by settling the issue of lordship and denying yourself. True discipleship is imparted. And the process can feel exacting, severe, and, at times, rigid, yet it is without controlling or overriding your free will. But, it is the only way to graduate to the orange belt level.

Cool Down Devotional Stretches:

I have sung all my life. And, all my life, my voice has been compared to the incomparable Luther Vandross who was one of my absolute favorite voices and vocalists. I remember vividly, when I stepped into lordship with Jesus Christ, that God clearly told me to set aside all my Luther Vandross albums and other balladeers alike because it led me into inordinate fantasy and lust.

What things in your life do you find yourself referencing with this statement, "That's really not that bad, it'll be okay"? What spiritual disciplines need to increase in your life to help you consistently exercise self-denial?

Chapter 4

Commitment

Chapter 4 - Orange Belt: Commitment

I remember the year 1991 so clearly. It was a very rare sunny day in Corvallis, Oregon where I completed my undergraduate work as well as some graduate work at Oregon State University. (Go Beavs!) While I was waiting at a traffic light, a very attractive girl crossed in front of my car. I can recall, as though it were yesterday, the thoughts that took place in my mind soon after seeing her. My eyes tracked her every move. The desire to know who she was intensified. Then it hit me—I have a girlfriend! Ironically, when I first met my girlfriend I had thought, "If I were to get her, I would be set and totally satisfied," because she was really good looking, or, like we said back in the day, "She was fine!" But in that moment, all of sudden, my eyes were wandering, and my girlfriend wasn't even in the framework of my mind. So sad.

The questions that came to my mind next were of the utmost importance: *How do you stay married to one person? How do you stay committed for the long haul?* After getting what I wanted, what I thought would satisfy me, I found myself in grave danger of repeating my family history— walking in a generational curse of broken commitments and infidelity.

Commitment is the act of pledging or engaging oneself to be obligated. That is why commitment is the foundation of true love, the kind of love that is bound by benevolence. This love is not motivated simply by feelings or emotion; it is spearheaded by choice. "But God demonstrated His own love toward us, in that while we were yet sinners, Christ died for us!"[1] That is why the traditional marriage ceremony is not only filled with declarations of undying love and emotions but also of unwavering commitment.

We have all had life-altering experiences with commitment, or the lack thereof. In the book of 1 Timothy, the Apostle Paul references how Timothy was raised. First, he references the sincere, genuine faith that was in his grandmother and mother. Second, Paul emphasizes the impartation of God's Word. There was both a modeling and an impartation of life—kind of sounds like discipleship to me. There was a generational impartation that took place. A legacy of the life of Christ was passed on to Timothy.

This became crucial for me. The virtue of being committed to my children was downloaded into me through my mother's displayed commitment across my whole life. How to be married was not! All I knew was that I didn't ever want to get divorced. My wife grew up not wanting to experience the heartache of divorce that her mother and mine did. Commitment to marriage was not a priority of our fathers. Now, I don't say this to rake our fathers over the coals. We love our fathers, but it doesn't negate what they did or the unfortunate effects their choices had on us.

Whether we are willing to admit it or not, most

1 - Rom. 5:8

people in this generation are closet commitment-phobes and have difficulty staying committed for the long term. We are scared! And the real problem for us in our walk with God is that, deep down, we question whether or not God is truly committed to us.

Even if you make a casual inquiry into the Bible, you cannot help but recognize that God puts a premium on commitment. Just look at how many times He refers to the nation of Israel as unfaithful, adulterers, or harlots. Listen to the words to the church at Laodicea: "I know your deeds, that you are neither cold nor hot; I wish that you were cold or hot. So because you are lukewarm, and neither hot nor cold, I will spit you out of My mouth."[2] What we find then is the crucial conditional statement in Luke chapter nine that puts the responsibility of being a disciple squarely in our laps. It is the combination of settling the issue, self-denial, and commitment being exercised into our nature, along with His power in our lives, that enables us to meet the daily requirements of His purposes. So, what is the first step God is looking for us to take after deciding to become committed to Him?

Jesus gives an invitation: "And He said to another, 'Follow Me.' But he said, 'Lord, permit me first to go and bury my father.' But He said to him, 'Allow the dead to bury their own dead; but as for you, go and proclaim everywhere the kingdom of God.'"[3] At first glance most people are like, "Wow, Jesus! Really? The man can't have compassion and go bury his father? What's up with that?" There are a few places a person could land when trying to decipher this encounter. First, he may have

2 - Rev. 3:15-16
3 - Lk. 9:59-60

wanted to fulfill the oldest son's duty to bury the father, to be near the father to ensure traditionally that he obtain an inheritance. Next, it could have been his desire to remain near the body of his father for up to one year to rebury the bones to keep up with cultural mores, a practice of some Jews at the time. Or, it could have been the excuses of a commitment-phobe. In this exchange, Jesus makes the statement to "let the dead bury the dead" so as to say, "do not let other things override your spiritual responsibilities, but, instead, be about the things of the kingdom of God!" I really believe the summation of Jesus' response here was that we cannot allow cultural standards and traditions to be more deeply embedded into our nature than the things of the kingdom of God!

In ancient Jewish culture, children, especially the eldest son, were duty-bound to take care of their parents. But here Jesus is unveiling that His call to discipleship, church building, and kingdom advancement supersedes all else—even that which would have been seen as the most important of traditions and cultural mores. Commitment always requires us to reprioritize.

When Jesus encountered the rich young ruler in Luke chapter 18, He tried to get the rich young ruler to reprioritize that which was most important to him in his life, but the young man refused and walked away from Jesus instead of following Him and becoming His disciple. Another passage reads:

Now large crowds were going along with Him; and He turned and said to them, "If anyone comes to Me, and does not hate his own father

*and mother and wife and children and brothers
and sisters, yes, and even his own life, he cannot
be My disciple. Whoever does not carry his own
cross and come after Me cannot be My disciple.*"[4]

Later on in the conversation, Jesus tells His
disciples they won't even be able to contain the blessings
coming their way because they reprioritized their lives.

Commitment is required to gain anything of great
value in life. The Bible says, "Everyone who competes in
the games exercises self-control in all things..."[5] Although
the expression *self-control* is used, it is done so with the
understanding that self-control and commitment run
on parallel tracks. You will not practice self-control if
there is nothing to be committed to. The self-control
necessary for achievement can be exercised only after
the commitment has been made.

The Bible also mentions some concepts that are
indelibly connected to commitment:

*Suffer hardship with me, as a good soldier
of Christ Jesus. No soldier in active service
entangles himself in the affairs of everyday
life, so that he may please the one who enlisted
him as a soldier. Also, if anyone competes as
an athlete, he does not win the prize unless he
competes according to the rules. The hard-
working farmer ought to be the first to receive
his share of the crops. Consider what I say,
for the Lord will give you understanding in*

4 - Lk. 14:25-27
5 - 1 Cor. 9:25

everything.[6]

To *suffer hardship* with someone implies commitment to that person and what they are suffering beneath. If you want to meet another person's needs, play according to certain rules, or work hard at anything, it requires commitment. David, the psalmist, expressed the need for a commitment to the fear of the Lord in order to develop true understanding and wisdom: "Who understands the power of Your anger and Your fury, according to the fear that is due You? So teach us to number our days, that we may present to You a heart of wisdom."[7] Commit to walking each day in the fear of the Lord as you should, and you will be set on the path to becoming a top-notch disciple-maker in the kingdom of God.

What if we committed to reprioritizing every area of our lives, would our witness at our jobs, schools, or gyms be louder in word and deed? Would the dimmer on our light in Christ be turned up? Would we be better prepared for marriage and have marriages worth emulating? Maybe, just maybe, we might raise a Timothy or two, perhaps we might even initiate a generational transference, building a powerful legacy of disciples. If you ever want things to change, you've got to do something different. Commitment demands that we reprioritize. If we don't, then we may begin to feel bogged down in our quest to attain the green belt level. And without being committed, the next step, being focused, can start to feel like a virtual impossibility.

6 - 2 Tim. 2:3-7
7 - Ps. 90:11-12

Cool Down Devotional Stretches:

After almost three decades of ministry, you can imagine that my wife and I have experienced many different scenarios and difficult seasons. I recall a two-year period where we were on staff at a particular church. The first year was great. Although the lead pastors had wonderful hearts and intentions, early in the second year I noticed a glaring weakness in their leadership style as they used control to get what they wanted from other staff, volunteers, and members in the church. I had initially committed to a minimum of two years when a reevaluation of my employment was to take place. I was suffocating and wanted to leave in that second year, BUT I had given my word! The Bible asks a question in Psalm 15:1b "Who shall dwell on your holy hill?" The writer of this psalm gave several descriptions to answer that question, one being "...who swears to his own hurt and does not change."[8]

Time for some self-reflection. Turn around in time and look back over your walk with God. Have you been committed to God first in all of your actions, even to your own pain? As is likely with all of us, our commitment sometimes fluctuates according to the condition and temperature of our circumstances—what steps do you need to take to sure up the principle of commitment in your life?

8 - Ps. 15:4c (ESV)

Chapter 5

Focus

Chapter 5 - Green Belt: Focus

As we look back over the first three components of becoming a black belt disciple-maker—lordship, self-denial, and commitment—this next component becomes a sort of litmus test for our progress in the journey. It is a place where we can begin to gauge our walk with Christ and assess areas of improvement that need to be made. Without unwavering focus while on our journey of becoming like Christ, and in becoming black belt disciple-makers, our journey can become cluttered with unneccesary obstacles.

Years ago I watched a Mel Gibson movie called *The Patriot*. This intense movie carried central themes of family values, integrity, honor, justice, and war. In one scene, Mel Gibson's character was reminding his three remaining sons, after losing one son only moments earlier due to a villain's cruelty, what their mother always used to tell them: "Stay the course."

We have all experienced times of distraction in our lives. Sometimes they are very much needed in light of the intensity of life, as a sort of respite, a breather if you will. But, many times, distractions are due to a lack of focus or proper weight given to the task at hand. Habakkuk says, "Record the vision and inscribe it on tablets, that the one who reads it may run. For the vision is yet for the appointed time; it hastens toward the goal and it will not fail. Though it tarries, wait for it; for it will certainly come, it will not delay.'"[1]

As you delve into this passage of Scripture a little deeper, you see the not-so-subtle hints interwoven. For instance, there is an "appointed time" for the vision to come to pass. No matter how long it "tarries" or takes, you must keep believing. It will "not delay." Even when you think the vision is developing too slowly, it is not. The destiny and plan of God for your life will certainly happen in God's perfect timetable. Stay focused and persevere. The word *wait* often sounds like a cuss word to us. But let me interpret that passage of Scripture another way: Lack of focus will always sabotage your productivity and derail your destiny.

A man who struggled with focus said to Jesus, "'I will follow You, Lord; but first permit me to say good-bye to those at home.' But Jesus said to him, 'No one, after putting his hand to the plow and looking back, is fit for the kingdom of God.'"[2] In other words, whoever takes on the particular task of becoming a disciple without the proper mindset, with a cavalier approach, is in danger of disqualification. The physical act here of looking back is a clear reference to being double-minded. Our hearts must be completely focused on the will of God. This is how the book of James addresses the issue:

> *But if any of you lacks wisdom, let him ask of*
> *God, who gives to all generously and without*
> *reproach, and it will be given to him. But he must*
> *ask in faith without any doubting, for the one*
> *who doubts is like the surf of the sea, driven*

1 - Hab. 2:2-3
2 - Lk. 9:57-62

and tossed by the wind. For that man ought not to expect that he will receive anything from the Lord, being a double-minded man, unstable in all his ways.[3]

Another passage reads:

For the eyes of the LORD move to and fro throughout the earth that He may strongly support those whose heart is completely His. You have acted foolishly in this. Indeed, from now on you will surely have wars.[4]

In this particular account in the Bible, Hanani, the prophet, came to Asa, the king of Judah. Hanani showed King Asa the contrast of what happened in the king's life when his heart and eyes were fixed on God, when he defeated the Ethiopians and the Lubim, a much larger and fiercer army, compared to when King Asa's heart became divided, and his eyes wavered. God informed him through the prophet that he had acted foolishly, and that, from that point forward, his portion would surely be wars. Make no mistake about it. Unnecessary spiritual warfar will be our portion too if we give the enemy access to our lives.

Let me emphasize something here: we are not talking about salvation, but relational discipleship. It would be unreasonable for my wife and me to expect our five daughters to contribute, naturally or spiritually, to this world if we did not train them and help get them fit to serve and please God.

3 - Js. 1:5-8
4 - 2 Chron. 16:9

I played professional football for a short time. Those who have played professional football know that if you come to training camp out of shape, you get fined. We were fined $250 a day or more until we met our required playing weight. And it's a good thing the regular season didn't start the week after our arrival at camp. The coach wouldn't have been able to play us because we weren't fit, suitable, useful, or qualified to play. And, if he did put us in the game unfit, most likely, we would get injured. God wants us able to handle the things of His kingdom, but to do that we have to be fit.

In biblical times, the tools that a farmer used were precious in his sight. In Luke chapter nine, we see how the plow was one of those immensely important tools to a farmer's ability to make a living and meet the needs of his family, in fact to their literal survival. There were no warehouse-sized hardware stores in Judea or a "Jerusalem Depot" that he could just run to and grab a replacement for a broken tool. There was just a local blacksmith with a line out the door and around the proverbial corner.

The blade on the plow was the most important part of the tool. It was extremely important for one to stay focused to make sure they did not hit a major rock or obstacle in the ground which could sabotage their ability to farm and be productive. Our job as disciples is to stay focused, avoid distractions, and not get derailed so that we can reach the harvest and help them become disciple-makers. Remember, if you are not fit, you are unqualified to make disciples; you cannot and will not be or produce something you are not.

Green Belt: Focus

Earlier, I said a football player who was not focused, who was unfit, was susceptible to injury if he played in a game. I remember getting injured as a fourteen-year-old, unable to travel with my all-star baseball team due to a lack of focus brought about by my disobedience. I, literally, almost lost my eye!

It was a beautiful June day in Denver, Colorado. My mother asked me to wash my bedroom walls. I thought to myself, "Really? It's eighty-degrees outside, and I need to work on this all-star pitching arm that God gave me. I'll practice my pitching against the side of the house!" Needless to say, I washed the walls so fast that you could barely feel the slightest layer of water on them. Out the door I went while my mother was on the phone talking to her friend. I could hear the question ringing in the air: "Ginooo, did you finish washing all those walls?" I yelled back, "Yesss, mother. I finished all of the walls!" I was free!

Well, about ten minutes into perfecting my pitches against the wall, the ball popped over our backyard fence. The gate to our fence had a hole in it that our dog used to squeeze through to escape from the backyard. Rather than fixing the gate, we moved my cement-filled tire, broken-off tetherball pole up against the hole in the fence so the dog couldn't get out.

Since I was already in a corner-cutting mood, evident by my speedy wall-washing job, I thought, "Why change things up now?" So, instead of moving the broken-off tetherball pole from the gate, I just tipped it over on its side to brace myself and jumped over the fence to grab the baseball. Well, it worked so well the first time, I figured I'd do it again. So, I hopped up on the fence, tipped the tetherball pole over on its side, jumped off the fence, landed on my feet while letting go of the pole. As I lifted my head, the pole, having a very jagged edge, ricocheted back and hit me in the corner of my eye—ouch! Immediately, I put my hand over my eye and covered it up. I thought, "Oh, it's wet. My eye must be watering because it got hit?" Then I saw the blood.

I can still remember the spine-tingling yell for my mother that scorched the skies that afternoon, as well as the hyperventilating, vomiting, and shock from that traumatizing event. I begged to play the rest of that summer with one eye, but to no avail. I suffered all summer long and missed out on the fruits of my hard work because of my lack of focus regarding the broken-off tetherball pole, not to mention the lackluster effort put forth in obeying my mom. As a child, I couldn't help but think over and over again that if I had done what I was supposed to do, that would have never happened to me. Most of the bad or unfortunate things that happen to us are because of our lack of focus. My destiny to play all-star baseball that summer was derailed because of my lack of focus, and my productivity was sabotaged as well.

There is a pretty prophetic picture of this when you study the story of Samson in the book of Judges. The Philistines gouged out both of Samson's eyes because of his lack of focus on the right things. Samson was called to be a judge and protector of God's people, Israel. But his life ended much earlier than it should have. He is a picture-perfect model of someone whose destiny was derailed and productivity was sabotaged. His headstone read, "I killed more of God's enemies in my death than I did while I was living." Tragically, he lost focus when it came to being one of God's disciples. It reminds me of how Anakin Skywalker killed the emperor, along with himself, in the movie *Return of the Jedi*. Instead of leading the Jedi alongside his son, Luke Skywalker, Anakin lost focus when he was a young Jedi disciple. Therefore, he missed out on a relationship with his children, Luke and Princess Leia.

How can we avoid becoming like one of those examples? A good place to start is by doing what Jesus said to do "Seek first His kingdom and His righteousness, and all these things will be added to you." Move beyond our often cliché approach and think of this scripture in this way, "But seek first His [*way of doing things*] and His [*way of being*], and all these things will be added to you."[5]

The Apostle Paul tells us in Hebrews 12 to look to our examples of successful disciples, get rid of our distractions, stay committed to our lane, fixate on worshiping Jesus, and, finally, have a good attitude in regards to the cross that He's called us to bear. Don't devalue it because it might not look or feel as glamorous as you would like. In the end, there is a place of honor waiting for you. When we set our faces like flint and give ourselves to unwavering focus like Jesus, the possibilities become endless, and our journey to the Blue Belt level becomes more than doable.

Cool Down Devotional Stretches:

Trouble and weeds thrive on a lack of attention. To pay attention, you must focus. Michelle and I often tell our kids, "You need to make important what Mommy and Daddy deem important." Jesus did, He said "Truly, truly, I say to

5 - Mt. 6:33 [emphasis mine]

you, the Son can do nothing of His own accord, but only what He *SEES* the Father doing."[6] To focus means that we look upon something until it becomes clear.

Time for a spiritual eye examination. Put the book down and engage your mind's eye. Now that we are almost halfway through the book, what subjects have we addressed that you need to bring into focus? How do the lenses in your spiritual goggles need to be adjusted? Whose help might you need to enlist to help strengthen your eye muscles?

6 - Jn. 5:19a (ESV)

Green Belt: Focus

Chapter 6

Accountability

Black Belt Descipleship

Chapter 6 - Blue Belt: Accountability

What you are willing to become in life will determine what you are willing to endure and whether or not you have what it takes. Now, there are goals you may have in the natural that no matter how willing you are—forget about it. They are not going to happen. You are just not going to become LeBron James, Peyton Manning, Michael Phelps, Stephen Curry, Carrie Underwood, Stevie Wonder, or William James Sidis (highest IQ in the world). Or, who knows, you just might be the person who comes along after these great talents to fill their shoes in a unique way. Either way, we are not talking about natural feats, but spiritual feats. These spiritual achievements are solely based upon us walking in a covenant with God that is undergirded by His grace and coupled with our faith.

Discipleship and disciple-making are covenant concepts in God's eyes. Becoming a trained, qualified, whole-hearted follower is not about the application of information, but the impartation of a life—Jesus' life. That is no easy task. It has to be based on covenant and it has to cost us something so that it will be meaningful. Maybe it will cost us everything so that it will become a conviction in our lives and not merely a preference when it is convenient for us.

When it comes to becoming a disciple, or

making disciples, convenience is not the norm. It wasn't convenient for Elisha in 1 Kings 19. Elijah came and found him and gave him God's personal invitation to be discipled. Elisha was to become God's prophet and, eventually, take Elijah's place. I mean, the call had to be exciting and scary all at the same time, but it was definitely not convenient. Elijah's successor had to make some hard decisions. The first was to settle the lordship issue.

For all intents and purposes, it appeared as though Elisha was headed for a pretty comfortable life. He owned, or was at least set to inherit, twelve yokes of oxen, not just twelve oxen, but at least twenty-four oxen to plow their land, and anybody else's for that matter. Elisha had a serious choice set before him. He could either continue walking in the life he was building for himself or he could walk into the greater calling that God had in store for him—one was very familiar and comfortable, while the other was riddled with unknowns. Elisha not only chose God, but made a bold statement by burning his yokes and oxen and celebrating with friends and family before joining Elijah in this new adventure with God!

In the next four chapters, we are going to look at a concept called "The Four Pit Stops of Discipleship." This was a process that was imparted to me through Pastor Jim Laffoon, with whom I have walked since 1994. Jim also fathered me in the prophetic office, so the lenses of these chapters will be colored through that of a prophetic nature. For the sake of continuity and the running metaphor of this book, I will refer to these "pit stops" as "Discipleship Dojos" or, simply, "Dojos." A *dojo* is where training takes place. I have attached the first discipleship dojo stop to the blue belt level of discipleship.

Blue Belt: Accountability

For Elisha, it was like any other day. Rise and shine; it was time to plow the land. He had no idea that this day would change his life forever. The sun was blazing and he was hard at work, sweating as usual, driving the oxen. Then, all of sudden, someone he didn't know, except by that person's incredible accomplishments, tossed his mantle upon Elisha. Unlike many of us at times, Elisha was clued in enough to recognize the significance of the moment. This wasn't some guy having a heatstroke, doing something weird; it was an opportunity for something unique to take place in Elisha's life. Elisha recognized God's fingerprints all over this otherwise random act.

God was calling Elisha to a new way of living, indicated by Elijah's comments to Elisha's reaction to the mantle being thrown on him: "He left the oxen and ran after Elijah and said, 'Please let me kiss my father and my mother, then I will follow you.' And he [Elijah] said to him, 'Go back again, for what have I done to you?'"[1] The nature of Elijah's response carries a very similar tone to Jesus' response to those in the Luke 9:57-62 passage. Now some might say all Elijah was saying was, "I am not saying you can't tie up your affairs and say goodbye to loved ones. Go right ahead, but just don't take too long!" And that could very well be true. But I think if you look a little deeper, you will see that Elijah was not referring to *goodbyes* as much as he was referring to *who* had called Elisha. It was not Elijah, but God.

First of all, it wasn't like Elijah's invitation came all wrapped up like a nice, neat, and elegant wedding invitation. No, Elijah threw the mantle and didn't even bother to slow down a bit to check Elisha's response.

1 - 1 Kgs. 19:20

Elisha had to run to catch up to Elijah. And if you know anything about Elijah, you know he could move pretty fast when he wanted to. How many people do you know who can outrun a chariot strapped to a couple of horses, as it was told of Elijah?[2] I didn't think so! Secondly, Elisha probably said to himself, "Elijah's been known to disappear for days at a time. So I better go make it crystal clear—I'm all in!"

After Elisha partied with his friends and family, he was off on the adventure of his life, or so he thought. "Then he left and followed Elijah, becoming his right-hand man."[3] Other versions say that Elisha ministered to Elijah, becoming his assistant and tending to his needs. At first glance, that doesn't sound too adventuresome, but more servile in nature. But that is exactly how God's process works. Most times we think, "Great, I'm gonna get discipled and learn how to prophesy the paint off the walls, get everyone healed, and preach the most faith-filled messages ever!" We focus on the anointing, which God gives liberally "...for He gives the Spirit without measure."[4] But God focuses on something else—covenant and character.

Gilgal

Unfortunately, there are so many things we do that do not tap into the biblical discipleship process because we have been conditioned by our westernized mindset of learning. We are top-heavy on the information-gathering side of the coin and anemic on the implementation side.

2 - 1 Kgs. 18:46 (NASB)
3 - 1 Kgs. 19:21 (The Message)
4 - Jn. 3:34b (ESV)

So, we'd do well to recognize that if God gives His Spirit, His anointing without measure, then He's probably more concerned with us understanding and getting what it takes to sustain that anointing, and actually being well-versed in what it takes to steward what the Holy Spirit is giving us and doing through us.

The first time we hear of the town of Gilgal in connection with Elijah and Elisha takes place a few days before God is going to take Elijah up to heaven in a fiery chariot. But it was not a place unfamiliar to Elisha. The last four places where Elijah and Elisha spent time together were Gilgal, Bethel, Jericho, and the River Jordan. They had frequented these places during their six to eight year discipleship relationship because those were the places that the schools of prophets whom Elijah trained inhabited. So, naturally, these places had significant spiritual meanings.

In 2 Kings chapter two, we are informed that God is about to take Elijah up to heaven very soon and that the prophet and his disciple (and prophet in training) were stationed in Gilgal at the time. We just found out that Elijah is about to make a spectacular exit from this planet. But, as you start to move through the chapter, you almost can't help asking yourself, "Why is Elijah stopping at these four places?" There is no reason on the surface to think of Gilgal as being significant unless you happen to know the history of Gilgal.

Gilgal is the place where the twelve stones taken from the Jordan River were set up to memorialize God's bringing of the children of Israel from the wilderness into the Promised Land and God's drying up of the Jordan

River for His people to cross over, causing the hearts of the kings of the Amorites and Canaanites to fade until "there was no longer any spirit in them because of the people of Israel."[5] *Gilgal* means liberty, a cutting or rolling away. This was the place where God's reinstitution of the rite of circumcision took place. God *cut a covenant* with Israel as they entered into the Promised Land.

Everything God does and has done in history is based on His covenant. Everything God has called us to do has been based on His covenant. Elisha knew what Gilgal represented. He wasn't the least bit clueless as to what had taken place there with his ancestors:

> *This is the reason why Joshua circumcised them: all the people who came out of Egypt who were males, all the men of war, died in the wilderness along the way after they came out of Egypt. For all the people who came out were circumcised, but all the people who were born in the wilderness along the way as they came out of Egypt had not been circumcised. For the sons of Israel walked forty years in the wilderness, until all the nation, that is, the men of war who came out of Egypt, perished because they did not listen to the voice of the Lord, to whom the Lord had sworn that He would not let them see the land which the Lord had sworn to their fathers to give us, a land flowing with milk and honey. Their children whom He raised up in their place, Joshua circumcised; for they were uncircumcised, because they had not*

5 - Josh. 5:1

circumcised them along the way.[6]

These people that had just crossed over into the Promised Land were a people of promise, but not a people of covenant or war—at least not yet. They needed to become a people of covenant in order to claim the promises of God and to win the wars that God would later have them engage in. The potential of a promise is not enough. It has to be ratified, made legal and official, and that is done through covenant.

Elisha, like everyone else, when reflecting upon the history of Gilgal, could only begin to imagine the pain felt by those men. (Talk about a good time to be a woman!) When he started following Elijah and they made their first trip to Gilgal, I'm sure Elisha was not taken aback when Elijah brought up the concept of covenant. The more pressing issue was how Elisha responded to Elijah the first time Elijah implied, "I gotta cutcha!" Another way of saying it is "Elisha, you're gonna need to let me cut into the vulnerable, insecure, sensitive areas of your life, so that you can receive healing and be strengthened." The book of Hebrews tells us, "For the word of God is living and active and sharper than any two-edged sword, and piercing as far as the division of soul and spirit, of both joints and marrow, and able to judge the thoughts and intentions of the heart."[7] The word of God cuts us with one edge of the sword and with the other He heals and strengthens us.

Elijah was letting Elisha know that this process was about much more than just gathering information and

6 - Josh. 5:4-7
7 - Heb. 4:12

learning how to do something. It was about imparting the nature of a disciple and, in Elisha's case, a prophet as well.

Think about it. When you were growing up, did someone sit you down and teach you about culture, or did you just pick it up and start walking in it? Did someone sit you down and teach you slang? Or, how about this one, did someone sit you in a classroom and teach you how to cuss like a sailor? I don't think so. No—it was *caught*! Now, I know we can sit in classrooms and learn about cultures, but we didn't sit in classrooms to learn about the culture we grew up in. Simply put, the important things Elisha needed, he had to *catch* from Elijah. The question always becomes, *can you trust someone to cut on you*?

The Two-fold Purpose in the Cutting Process

What we need to remember is that everything about the life of a disciple is based on a covenant established through the shedding of the blood of Jesus on the cross. There are two aspects of the spiritual cutting process, and they are both reliant on a covenant. In the Old Testament of the Bible, physical circumcision represented the covenant with God. The New Testament says that "circumcision is that which is of the heart, by the Spirit, not by the letter..."[8] So, the New Testament covenant is cut, ratified, by a spiritual circumcision of the heart taking place. But, whether Old Testament or New Testament, the outcome is the same—you become a disciple through a transformed life by obeying and trusting God. Let's take a look at these two aspects of the "Gilgal Process."

1. **Circumcision**: The people who were born in

8 - Rom. 2:29

the wilderness after leaving Egypt had not been circumcised on the way. It was as though they had been in a birthing process, came out, crossed over the Jordan River, and then the maturation process began. And once they had come under lordship, denied themselves, become committed, and got focused, the next step was to be cut on. They allowed Joshua and Caleb to cut them and roll back the foreskin to expose the vulnerable, sensitive, hurt areas that Egypt (symbolic of sin and bondage) and the missteps of their parents had caused in their lives, thereby enabling God's healing process to take place. "*Now when they had finished circumcising all the nation, they remained in their places in the camp until they were healed. Then the LORD said to Joshua, 'Today I have rolled away the reproach of Egypt from you.' So the name of that place is called Gilgal to this day.*"[9] The same steps should take place today among disciples and disciple-makers. Those in the healing process should be protected and watched over by those who have already gone through the Gilgal Process.

2. **Spiritual** Warfare: This is also a time of preparation for war. This is where the warriors of God are made in the spirit and taught how to fight by trusting God. Other than Joshua and Caleb, they were at their most vulnerable point as a nation during this part of the process. While in a debilitative state following the circumcision, they had to trust two men in their eighties who were surrounded by women. But you have to go through these types of seasons of vulnerability in order

9 - Josh. 5:8-9

to fully mature. This maturation process not only requires you to put your trust in God, but also in those He has called to lead you and walk with you.

I find it quite interesting that when Jesus talks about the process of discipleship, He uses the analogies of *building a tower* and a *king going out to battle.*[10] And He clearly states that if you don't embrace the process of being vulnerable and trusting Him, "...then, none of you can be My disciple..."[11]

A good indicator that we are on the road to maturity as a disciple is when we can answer these two questions positively:

1.   Can I follow someone (after salvation)?

These men had to trust Joshua now, but could they? It was easier said than done.

2.   Can I trust someone to cut on me?

Israel had to trust God's process even when it looked unfavorable in the natural.

When we can answer *yes* to these questions and embrace this process, our lives start to become a powerful force and an example to others. If we want to be the disciples God has called us to be, we simply cannot forgo any of the dojo stops of discipleship. This dojo stop primes the pump for us to move on to the next dojo stop, the purple belt level of disciple-making.

10 - Lk. 14:25-33
11 - Lk. 14:33

Cool Down Devotional Stretches:

I have five daughters and, as parents, we all want to pass on the good attributes we have...especially spiritually. But, as it turns out, I passed on my athletic prowess to them as well. All of my daughters are exceptional athletes and competitive soccer players who dream of playing D-1 soccer and beyond. I have a dear friend who trains them, I call him a "soccer savant." Many times, they come home from training "butt-hurt (LOL)" because of the way Coach Mike corrected them. I tell them, "Coach Mike doesn't coddle, he develops--(in love) he's like the pressure applied to the coal that produces the diamond (ouch)!" Jesus, in love, spoke some tough things to His disciples such as, "Truly, truly, I say to you, unless you eat the flesh of the Son of Man and drink His blood, you have no life in you."[12] I love it because I'm not a part of the "Pillsbury Doughboy" generation we live in now. To become what you truly desire, you cannot be afraid to face the pressure.

Time to go get a spiritual body composition. Are you spiritually soft or firm when being corrected and held accountable in your walk with God? Are you more concerned about the delivery or the content of the correction coming your way? What if God brings someone in your life whose personality doesn't jive with yours, can you still receive correction from them?

12 - Jn. 6:53 (ESV)

Chapter 7

Worship

Chapter 7 - Purple Belt: Worship

Peter, discerning that his time on earth was drawing to a close, had this to say:

> *Therefore, I will always be ready to remind you of these things, even though you already know them, and have been established in the truth which is present with you. I consider it right, as long as I am in this earthly dwelling, to stir you up by way of reminder, knowing that the laying aside of my earthly dwelling is imminent, as also our Lord Jesus Christ has made clear to me. And I will also be diligent that at any time after my departure you will be able to call these things to mind.[1]*

It would appear that this was what Elijah did with Elisha. He took the time to remind Elisha of what he had learned in those important places while they retraced the steps of Elijah's prophetic circuit before his departure. That circuit would soon become Elisha's as he stepped into Elijah's role overseeing the school of the prophets. Being a disciple is no walk in the park. And learning how to worship in the house of God is one of the most important building blocks needed for a strong foundation in our walk with God. This particular dojo stop is all about that.

1 - 1 Pet. 1:12-15

When I say "worship in the house of God" I am not referring to a particular building or edifice. Under the New Testament, we are the temple of God where He chooses to dwell: "You also, as living stones, are being built up as a spiritual house for a holy priesthood, to offer up spiritual sacrifices acceptable to God through Jesus Christ."[2] When Jesus encountered the woman at the well, He went on to explain to her that the manifestation and expression of worship were about to change:

> *The woman said to Him, "Sir, I perceive that You are a prophet. Our fathers worshiped in this mountain, and you people say that in Jerusalem is the place where men ought to worship." Jesus said to her, "Woman, believe Me, an hour is coming when neither in this mountain nor in Jerusalem will you worship the Father. You worship what you do not know; we worship what we know, for salvation is from the Jews. But an hour is coming, and now is, when the true worshipers will worship the Father in spirit and truth; for such people the Father seeks to be His worshipers. God is spirit, and those who worship Him must worship in spirit and truth."[3]*

Jesus tells her that they worship what they "do not know." In other words, you worship someone that you are not intimate with. Jesus begins to explain that their religious rituals are about to be done away with, and they are going to learn the real way to worship, which is "in spirit and truth." And, as they pursue spirit and truth, it

2 - 1 Pet. 2:5
3 - Jn. 4:19-24

will produce an intimacy, a relationship with the Father, that trumps religiosity. So, when I say worship in the *house of God*, I'm referring to how one relates in unity to the family of God and gives his or her entire life as worship unto God.

As we talk about pursuing spirit and truth, we are venturing into the area of finding and practicing the presence of God. We don't like to admit it, but most of the time we struggle in our efforts to enter into His presence. Sometimes we feel lost in our ability to hear Him or sense His presence. Well, I want to tell you: we are not alone. People in the Bible struggled with it too. Whether you believe it or not, there is an art to finding God's presence. The Bible is riddled with instructions on how to approach Him. There is a way, not a scientific formula, not a mathematical equation, but a *way* to finding God's presence. Some call it devotion. Some might call it face time. Simpy put, it is a form of worship.

One of the main reasons we go to church is to worship. We go to deepen our relationships with God and the spiritual family He has joined us with. And, as we build our personal relationship with God, we enhance our ability to build in this family. These two aspects are like the parallel rails of a train track. If you are not going deep in your relationship with God, then it is likely that things are going to be extremely shallow with the family of God. True growth in God allows for true growth with His family. It also allows for the opportunity to experience the manifold expressions of who He is in His people. But religiosity and counterfeit worship will always stifle that kind of growth. Elijah understood this. He knew he had to spend quality time with Elisha in Bethel to ensure Elisha didn't fall into the religious trap of feigned worship.

Overcoming Religiosity

One of the best stories of overcoming religiosity and walking into true worship is found in the narrative involving Jacob's journey in which God renames him *Israel*. We also learn from that passage that true transformation is found in the presence of God. In Genesis 28, we see Jacob using the word *Bethel*. Jacob seemed to have borrowed the word from an experience his grandfather Abraham had had with God.

Jacob was well acquainted with his grandfather's and father's journeys with God. There had been plenty of storytimes as Abraham recited his encounters with God—it was the Hebrew way. So, when Jacob had his supernatural dream involving a ladder with descending and ascending angels, it was not a stretch for him to mimic what Abraham did in Genesis 12 when God came and talked with Abraham.

After God told Abraham he was going to have many descendants, Abraham went to a mountain in Bethel and built an altar to the Lord and worshiped. When Jacob had his experience with God in the dream, he made the rock he slept on into an altar of worship to God and called that place Bethel. The major difference between these two stories was that one of them was very religious, and one was very relational.

Names in the Hebrew or Jewish culture are extremely important. Even the word *name* in the Hebrew and Greek means authority, standing, reputation, character, fame, or renown. At various times throughout the Bible, God changed a person's name due to a life transformation and the manifest destiny of God on their lives. The phrase *in the name of* actually means *in the standing, reputation, authority, character, fame, and renown of someone.* Jacob's name means *he who supplants, follows after, heels, trips up, takes hold by the hand, detains or swindles.* None of those descriptions are very flattering, to say the least! Obviously, it was not God's desire for Jacob to be a swindler. God had a plan.

Rewinding back in Jacob's story, we see that Jacob not only coaxed his brother, Esau, to give him his birthright, but Jacob also tricked their father, Isaac, into giving him the blessing of the firstborn, ultimately stealing what belonged to Esau. In light of this ruse, Jacob ended up with two choices—run away or risk death at the hand of his brother. Jacob put on his track shoes and got the heck outta dodge! To avoid Esau and his henchmen, Jacob's mom sent him back to Abraham's family. Along the way, while sleeping one night, God decided to visit Jacob in a dream. I believe God had to speak to him in a dream because of Jacob's nature. He might not have perceived that it was the Lord otherwise. This was evident by his comment, "Surely the Lord was in this place, and I didn't know it!"[4] Unlike Abraham, Jacob was not accustomed to recognizing the presence of God. The Lord told the two of them basically the same thing, but Jacob had to be told while asleep. God primarily spoke to Abraham while he was awake, or in what can be described as a vision—just something to chew on. God speaks to us in many different ways, taking our personalities, learning styles, and maturity with Him all into account.

4 - Gen. 25:31, 27:36, 28:16 (ESV)

I used to criticize Jacob for that statement he made and say of him, "How could you not recognize the presence of God in a place?" Then there were a couple of times that I didn't recognize the presence of God "in a place." My pride was exposed, and I realized that we all have some Jacob in us. I began to understand that we are all on Jacob's journey until we wrestle with God, and He changes our nature. We are all a religious hot mess!

It is interesting how God said, "I ...will bring you back to this land; for I will not leave you until I have done what I have promised you."[5] In other words, "Once I've changed your nature, I'll bring you back here to this land where the house of God is." It seems to be a running theme with God—just ask Abraham, Moses, Peter, and Gino. After He's taken you on this journey to change your nature, He'll bring you back to that which He originally called you to accomplish! We go from being *bricks* to *living stones* that become a part of a spiritual house of worship.

And the fact that we become a spiritual house of worship, I believe, is one of the reasons God encourages us not to forsake our assembling together:

So let's do it—full of belief, confident that we're presentable inside and out. Let's keep a firm grip on the promises that keep us going. He always keeps his word. Let's see how inventive we can be in encouraging love and helping out, not avoiding worshiping together as some do but spurring each other on, especially as we see the big Day approaching.[6]

5 - Gen. 28:15
6 - Heb. 10:22-25 (The Message)

Notice how the Word tells us to encourage and spur each other on. This is important in the backdrop of having the nature of a disciple imparted into oneself. If you are not constantly around those who have what you need, how else can it be imparted? How else can you catch *it*? To have religiosity knocked off of us and the real thing (relationship) downloaded into us, we have to be around it. I can hear you thinking, "God can impart it if He wants to!" And you're right. He can, but that's not generally His norm. In the Bible, there seems to be this recurring pattern of God mainly working through people to accomplish what He wants to be done. He allows us to become His children, in the family business, partnering with His purposes to bring about His glory.

Discipline of Devotion

During their frequent trips to Bethel, Elijah taught Elisha the importance of having a personal devotional time and building his friendship with God. Let us examine two stories regarding the correlation between the phrase "move [pitch] the tent" and the concept of worship through friendship or devotional time. The first one involves Abram (Abraham) and an encounter he has with God:

> *The LORD said to Abram, after Lot had separated from him, "Now lift up your eyes and look from the place where you are, northward and southward and eastward and westward; for all the land which you see, I will give it to you and to your descendants forever. I will make your descendants as the dust of the earth, so*

*that if anyone can number the dust of the earth,
then your descendants can also be numbered.
Arise, walk about the land through its length
and breadth; for I will give it to you." Then
Abram moved his tent and came and dwelt by
the oaks of Mamre, which are in Hebron, and
there he built an altar to the LORD.[7]*

At first, this all seems like normal stuff. The Lord
lets Abram choose where he wants to live. God gives it all
to him. And like most human beings stuck in a desert, you
pick the spot that might have the most shade because of
the trees. But I always believe there are little prophetic
nuggets to be found if you are willing to look deeply
enough. It turns out that *Mamre* means strength or vigor,
and *Hebron* means friendship or alliance. In essence, you
could say that Abram shaded himself with the strength
and friendship of God and worshiped Him in that place.
Some might say that's a stretch. But Abraham did spend
twenty plus years in Hebron after building an altar there
to worship. That is plenty of time to pitch your tent and
build a solid friendship—I'm just sayin'. And the Bible
does call Abraham a friend of God.[8] I am convinced that
this is where God friended, discipled, and imparted into
Abraham all he would need to become the father of our
faith. And all of this happened because he pitched his tent
in the right place!

This second story highlights the depth of
relationship possible for those who "pitch their tent" in
God's presence, building an intimate friendship with
Him. I remember hearing Jim Laffoon expound on the

7 - Gen. 13:14-18 (ESV)
8 - Isa. 41:8b

discipline of devotion, teaching out of the book of Exodus:

> *Now Moses used to take the tent and pitch it*
> *outside the camp, a good distance from the*
> *camp, and he called it the tent of meeting. And*
> *everyone who sought the LORD would go out to*
> *the tent of meeting which was outside the camp.*
> *And it came about, whenever Moses went out*
> *to the tent, that all the people would arise and*
> *stand, each at the entrance of his tent, and gaze*
> *after Moses until he entered the tent. Whenever*
> *Moses entered the tent, the pillar of cloud would*
> *descend and stand at the entrance of the tent;*
> *and the LORD would speak with Moses. When*
> *all the people saw the pillar of cloud standing*
> *at the entrance of the tent, all the people would*
> *arise and worship, each at the entrance of his*
> *tent. Thus the LORD used to speak to Moses face*
> *to face, just as a man speaks to his friend. When*
> *Moses returned to the camp, his servant Joshua,*
> *the son of Nun, a young man, would not depart*
> *from the tent.*[9]

Now before we continue, I think it's important to clarify what tent we're talking about. This is not referring to the Tabernacle that the children of Israel would set up whenever the "pillar of cloud" that would lead them by day or the "pillar of fire" that would lead them by night stopped. The Tabernacle was extensive; it had three sections to it, and each housed certain articles and utensils in them, the most important one being the "ark of the covenant" in the innermost court, which was called

9 - Ex. 33:7-11 (NASB)

the "holy of holies." The children of Israel would camp in a configuration comprised of four groups, each containing three tribes: one group facing the north side, one the south side, one the east side, and another the west side, all surrounding the Tabernacle. This was a beautiful picture and foreshadowing of how the Lord would one day dwell at the very core of our hearts...in the deepest and most intimate places of our being.

Let's focus on the first sentence, "Now Moses used to take the tent and pitch it outside the camp, a good distance from the camp, and he called it the tent of meeting."[10] This was not the place where sacrifices were made for sins, nor where ceremonial washings took place. No, this was the place, the tent, where you would go to get away from the noise and the crowd. This was where you headed to personally invite the presence of God to foster and build your relationship with the "Great I Am!"

In this passage, God takes a moment to give us a glimpse into the life of Moses and shows us what a personal relationship with Him and true worship ought to look like. This is a prophetic picture of what would be available to the body of Christ after Jesus' ascension into heaven. This wasn't the Tabernacle, but the "tent of meeting," a place for those who sought to meet with the Lord. This was not a place of religious rites and rituals, but a place to seek God, connect, and build relationally.

Let's look at the dynamics of this passage. Now, remember, this is during the wilderness time for the children of Israel, and the custom was that when the cloud of God moved in the daytime, or the pillar of fire by

10 - Ex. 33:7

night, the children of Israel would break camp, pack up, and move. So, this means that Moses would have to break down the tent of meeting and put it back up every time they moved...and then "pitch the tent" again wherever they stopped. Who knows the duration of stay they had at each stop. It could have been a couple of days, a week, a few months; there is simply no way of telling. But one thing is for sure—whatever the duration of stay was, Moses was sure to pitch the tent of meeting when they set up camp.

God would speak with Moses inside the tent. Moses would bring Joshua along so he could experience Moses' face time with God. Talk about some legit discipleship! And the experience was so good to Joshua that, even after Moses left, Joshua would not leave the tent. This was something all of Israel could do as frequently as they wanted to—no appointment needed.[11]

As we travel deeper into the passage, we find that not all responses from the people given the opportunity to go spend time with God one-on-one were the same. The people seemed content to worship God from the front of their own tent. In other words, they chose to worship God from afar. Not only that, but they also tried to live vicariously through the relationship that Moses and Joshua had with God.

Unfortunately, the same thing is happening in the church of America today. The congregation tries to live vicariously off of the anointing and relationship that the pastor (hopefully) has with God, only to find out that, like the children of Israel in the wilderness, they don't have

11 - Ex. 33:7

what it takes to pass the test. Barna Group[iv], a research and resource company, found that less than twenty percent of Americans read their Bible regularly. How could you possibly have a legitimate relationship with God and not even take the time to become intimate with Him?

Driving Home the Stakes

While the children of Israel wandered in the wilderness, they were protected during the day by the pillar of cloud and protected at night by the pillar of fire.[12] They moved when the pillar moved. Whenever the pillar stopped, they would set up camp. Moses would have had to break down the tent of meeting and put it back up every time they moved. He'd have to "pitch the tent" again wherever they stopped. What must it have looked like every time Moses went to pitch that tent of meeting? He would have placed the foundational center post. He would have centered the tent canvass. Next, he would have taken the four corner stakes and, with a hammering tool, driven them into the ground. And, lastly, Moses would have anchored everything down with the ropes. Sounds like quite the process to keep repeating over and over for forty years. I can't help but think that all those people watching him were saying to themselves, "Why doesn't he just stay in his own tent and meet with God? I'm sure the cloud could descend there just as easily, 'cuz that seems like a whole lotta trouble for a couple of hours or so."

Notice how Moses would go and pitch the tent outside of the camp—and for good reason. He had to get away from the crowd. As disciples of Christ, it is imperative that we get away from all of the distractions

12 - Ex. 3:21

of life and draw away to be with Him. We must practice this discipline of devotion. Jesus modeled this practice when He would often leave the crowds to go to a place of solitude and commune with the Father.

I want to focus on a really important concept that Pastor Jim Laffoon calls "Driving Home the Four Stakes of Devotion":

1. **Worship**: How we approach the presence of God is vitally important. The only way to truly approach Him is with a heart of reverence. This takes concentrated practice, especially when you don't physically see the person you are worshiping. Why do you think people throughout history have made idols out of wood and different metals? They made them because they could physically see them. Think about Moses' first encounter with God. The first thing God did was tell Moses to take off his shoes because he was standing on holy ground.[13] God was instilling the principle of reverence into the very fabric of Moses' nature. Ultimately, worship is about what you value. That which you value most in life you will worship.

2. **Word**: Moses did not have the Holy Bible to read like we have today. But what Moses did have were face-to-face encounters with God Himself. The Lord said, "I talk to Moses like a man talks to a friend!"[14] Now, some would say, "That's not fair! Why don't we get what Moses had?" Au contraire, mon frère! We absolutely get what Moses got!

13 - Ex. 3:5
14 - Ex. 33:11

Hebrews tells us, "For the word of God is living and active and sharper than any two-edged sword, and piercing as far as the division of soul and spirit, of both joints and marrow, and able to judge the thoughts and intentions of the heart."[15] Also, the Bible says, "In the beginning was the Word, and the Word was with God, and the Word was God. He was in the beginning with God...And the Word became flesh, and dwelt among us, and we saw His glory, glory as of the only begotten from the Father, full of grace and truth."[16] The *Logos* (or Word), who is Jesus, is ours for the having! He is more than available to us and longs to dwell with us as a friend and big brother in a loving relationship. And, many times in the Bible, Jesus references that He is the manifestation of who the Father is in character, nature, and spirit. Here is just one exchange regarding Jesus' oneness with the Father:

If you had known Me, you would have known My Father also; from now on you know Him, and have seen Him." Philip said to Him, "Lord, show us the Father, and it is enough for us." Jesus said to him, "Have I been so long with you, and yet you have not come to know Me, Philip? He who has seen Me has seen the Father; how can you say, 'Show us the Father?' Do you not believe that I am in the Father, and the Father is in Me? The words that I say to you I do not speak on My own initiative, but the Father abiding in

15 - Heb. 4:12
16 - Jn. 1:1-2, 14

Me does His works.[17]

It is essential to drive the stake of the Word into our spiritual foundation to know God the Father, Jesus, and the Holy Spirit. Ever since my early walk with the Lord, I have consistently prayed at the beginning of my devotional time that Jesus would do for me what he did for His disciples before He ascended into heaven, "Then He opened their minds to understand the Scriptures..."[18] Oh, that He would do the same for you as you become a black belt disciple-maker!

3. **Prayer**: This third stake is critical in the process— kind of a linchpin, if you will.
As we worship and meditate on the Word of God, prayer becomes the component that holds it all together. If we don't get the proper handle on prayer, then our attempts at driving home the fourth stake will be anemic at best. The New Testament is riddled with instructions and examples of how to pray. Those are primarily according to the will of God and in the name (character) of Jesus, which, by the way, you couldn't possibly know if you haven't become immensely intimate with God by meditating on His Word. A major passage of scripture regarding the will of God is found in the book of Matthew:

Pray, then, in this way: "Our Father who is in heaven, Hallowed be Your name. Your kingdom come. Your will be done, On earth as it is in heaven. Give us this day our daily bread. And

17 - Jn. 14:7-10
18 - Lk. 24:45a

*forgive us our debts, as we also have forgiven
our debtors. And do not lead us into temptation,
but deliver us from evil. [For Yours is the
kingdom and the power and the glory forever.
Amen."]*[19]

In regards to His name, "Whatever you ask in My name,
that will I do, so that the Father may be glorified in the Son.
If you ask Me anything in My name, I will do it."[20] And the
Bible also says, "In that day you will not question Me about
anything. Truly, truly, I say to you, if you ask the Father
for anything in My name, He will give it to you."[21] When
we pray this way, two things come into play: (1) God sends
His angels to minister on our behalf. "Bless the LORD, you
His angels, mighty in strength, who perform His word,
obeying the voice of His word!"[22] and (2) God does not go
back on His Word because He cannot deny Himself:

*For as the rain and the snow come down from
heaven, And do not return there without
watering the earth. And making it bear and
sprout, And furnishing seed to the sower and
bread to the eater; So will My word be which
goes forth from My mouth; It will not return to
Me empty, Without accomplishing what I desire,
And without succeeding in the matter for which
I sent it.*[23]

When we pray in this manner, something happens.

19 - Mt. 6:9-13
20 - Jn. 14:13-14
21 - Jn. 16:23
22 - Ps. 103:20
23 - Isa. 55:10-11

Our prayers move past the iron ceiling we might have experienced in the past and are catapulted into the heavens where the Father resides. But it doesn't stop there. The Word also tells us that Jesus sits at the right hand of the Father to intercede for us. "Therefore He is able also to save forever those who draw near to God through Him, since He always lives to make intercession for them."[24] Quite the deal, I'd say!

4. **Wait**: For many people, this last stake could be the hardest foundational stake to drive in. I know for me, it's a bear sometimes! There are a few reasons why. First, this is a relationship unlike any other relationship we have. We need to wait to have a conversation with someone we don't physically see or touch. Second, we are by nature tremendously impatient, a microwave-generation mentality. And third, it takes faith! But through frequent practice of being in God's presence, we can see and touch and hear Him in the spirit realm. By focusing on the rewards of spending time with God, we can relax and quiet our souls. And by faith, we can trust that the spirit realm is more real than the chair you sit in, the couch you relax on, or the bed you lie in. None of these realities are easily mastered. But once they are, the rewards are priceless.

Waiting on the Lord—to get quiet and intimate before God and talk with Him like a man talks with his friend— has always been my greatest desire as well as my greatest struggle. When my wife and I planted our first church as the lead pastors, we had to participate in an assessment

24 - Heb. 7:25

program to enable this particular church movement to gauge what we were like and what gifts we might move in, along with assessing our strengths and weaknesses. Part of the assessment required that we take a battery of tests administered by a psychologist and then, later on, we sat with him and reviewed the results together. The first thing out of his mouth was, "Well, you guys don't lie much, and you're not crazy!" (Good to know!) Then he laughed and explained that "Most Christians, when they take these tests stretch the truth a good bit because they don't want to look bad as Christians, but you guys don't do that!"

That was encouraging for Michelle and me to hear, but I also understand that it is almost humanly impossible to not want to be seen in the brightest light possible. The most encouraging thing I heard from him came later in the meeting when he got to the *manic* portion of our results. He looked at my wife and said, "Your numbers in this section were fine, everything was right in the middle." Then, he turned to me and said, "But you, your numbers were high, extremely high, but not in the danger zone. You're not manic depressive or anything like that. But your numbers are right at the top, right before there's need for concern." He looked at me and said, "You have an enormous amount of energy in your mind. Matter of fact, your mind is more manic than 80-90% of the men in the world!"

Now you might be wondering why that was encouraging to me. Well, for one thing, I realized I wasn't going crazy! The other thing is that it gave me insight into how God wired me and helped explain some of my past experiences. I remember, back in 1994, becoming extremely frustrated with my quiet time with the Lord.

So I called Jim Laffoon up and explained my frustration to him, "Pastor Jim, how do you quiet your soul to hear God? Every time I try, before you know it, I'm formulating a new message to preach in my head, or someone pops into my mind to pray for or to encourage with a passage of scripture. It's frustrating because I want this time to be for me with Him."

It's a priceless thing to be in a relationship with someone who has a legitimate and intimate relationship with the Father! Leave it up to Pastor Jim to not just give me some formula to work to perfection, but instead, something to drive me deeper into the discipline of *practicing the presence* of God! Jim's reply to my whining was this: "G-faith (his nickname for me), I understand exactly where you're at, my friend. It's one of the hardest disciplines to develop in our walk with God. Thank Him for the message, brotha, and then just sit there! Sometimes God just wants to know you want to be with Him without wanting something from Him!"

After that reply, this is what I said to myself, "OUCH! Stop steppin' on my toes man!" But then he told me to go meditate on Psalms 130 and 131. Then, he explained how, at age 23 and dying of hepatitis while in the jungle as a missionary, God had Him *wait* on Him— not just wait as in *biding time*, but as in the Hebrew word *Qâvâh* which means to *hope in; twist and bind like a tree's roots with other trees*. God had Jim *twist and bind* and put his expectation in Him for this dire, deathly situation! Jim then continued to share how, in his early thirties, he had developed Chronic Fatigue Syndrome and went home to live with his parents. While there, God told him to "Rest and wait on Me! Sit quietly before Me for a month. Don't read the Bible. Don't do anything. *Just* sit with Me!" Jim told me that that was the longest he ever went without reading his Bible, that God wouldn't even let him pray hard:

> *Out of the depths I have cried to You, O LORD.*
> *Lord, hear my voice! Let Your ears be attentive*
> *to the voice of my supplications. If You, LORD,*
> *should mark iniquities, O Lord, who could*
> *stand? But there is forgiveness with You, that*
> *You may be feared. I wait for the LORD, my soul*
> *does wait, and in His word do I hope. My soul*
> *waits for the Lord more than the watchmen for*
> *the morning; indeed, more than the watchmen*
> *for the morning. O Israel, hope in the LORD;*
> *for with the LORD there is lovingkindness, and*
> *with Him is abundant redemption. And He will*
> *redeem Israel from all his iniquities.*[25]

> *O LORD, my heart is not proud, nor my eyes*
> *haughty; nor do I involve myself in great*
> *matters, or in things too difficult for me. Surely*
> *I have composed and quieted my soul; like a*
> *weaned child rests against his mother, my soul is*
> *like a weaned child within me. O Israel, hope in*
> *the LORD from this time forth and forever.*[26]

During those times, God healed Jim of Hepatitis and Chronic Fatigue Syndrome. And, needless to say, Jim learned the art of practicing God's presence, too. Today, Jim is an extraordinary prophet in the body of Christ, touching nations and changing lives by the power of Jesus

25 - Ps. 130:1-8
26 - Ps. 131:1-3

Christ. And much of that is due to his relentless discipline of *pitching his tent* and pursuing an intimate relationship with his Heavenly Father.

What makes waiting on the Lord and practicing His presence so important? It brings you into a place where His *rhema* (spoken) words to you are frequent because you have come to know His *logos* (written) words so well. Jesus puts it this way, "If you abide in Me [*logos*], and My words [*rhema/rhemata*] abide in you, ask whatever you wish, and it will be done for you [*emphasis mine*]!"[27]

We are the temple of God. "Do you not know that you are a temple of God and that the Spirit of God dwells in you?"[28] The encouraging thing is that we don't have to carry a tent, foundational post, four stakes, rope, or a tool to pitch the tent with anymore. Nope, all we have to do now is find a quiet place and pitch *ourselves* wherever we are because He lives in us!

Imagine not being aware of His presence while He lives in you. It's like being in a room with someone sitting right next to you and you don't even know it—or worse, you ignore the person. Now, envision yourself building the kind of friendship with Your Heavenly Father that, when people get around you, it causes them to want what you got—unlimited access to Daddy's holy of holies, the inner court! Lastly, see yourself learning the art of being in God's presence and tapping into the process of being transformed into His image.

When combined, these *spiritual stakes*, which are essential and eminent to the foundation of your devotional

27 - Jn. 15:7 [emphasis mine]
28 - 1 Cor. 3:16

life, produce a synergism that will manifest the presence of God in your life. And, when practiced consistently, they will cause a spiritual magnetism that can be rejected by those in the world, but not denied. Abiding in His presence is for *you*. You walking in His presence is for *others*. True transformation is realized through intimacy with Him. Without this transforming relationship, there is no moving on to the brown-belt level of discipleship.

Cool Down Devotional Stretches:

If you observe human beings long enough, you will conclude that worship is embedded into the very fabric of our nature, our design. The Bible states, "For whatever overcomes a person, to that he is enslaved."[29] I have experienced this with food, lust, fear, and the like. I remember fudge marble Haagen-Dazs being that which I worshiped and gave myself over to. That was what I reached for to find comfort and soothe my emotional turmoil. Worship, at its very core, is all about what you value most and giving yourself over to it!

Okay, time to check under the hood and see if you need an oil change. Worship oils the soul! Worship is putting God first in all you do! Have you been allowing worship through the Holy Spirit to oil your soul and spirit, or have you been filling up on substitutes such as sex, money, pride, fear, intellect, family, physical fitness, success, or any other GMO version of satisfaction?

29 - 2 Pet. 2:19b (ESV)

Chapter 8

Sovereignty

Black Belt Descipleship

Chapter 8 - Brown Belt: Sovereignty

Sovereignty is when a person or thing has supreme power and authority. Absolute sovereignty belongs to God alone. Without pitching your tent and developing a truly intimate relationship with the Lord, it is going to be really hard to walk by faith in the sovereignty of God. And, as a disciple, it is a *must* that you believe in His sovereignty.

In light of what Elijah had personally experienced regarding the subject of sovereignty, he knew how vital it was for Elisha to learn the same lessons. Elijah encountered several situations where the need to trust God for provision, protection, and guidance was at a premium. Whether it was sitting by a brook trusting God to feed him with food brought to him by birds or trusting God to provide for a woman and child about to die of starvation, he was intimately acquainted with the sovereignty of God. Somehow, I never marveled at the fact that birds brought Elijah food, but that they never ate the food themselves blew my mind! It just confirmed Jesus' words: "Consider the ravens, for they neither sow nor reap; they have no storeroom nor barn, and yet God feeds them; how much more valuable you are than the birds!"[1] The birds knew their value and didn't worry about their provision, and neither should we. (I know, easier said than done.)

1 - Lk. 12:24

Whether we realize it or not, we all, at times, walk in some sense of limited sovereignty. We have the power to choose our friends. We choose our careers. When we make travel plans, we decide on what clothes to bring, the food we might eat, and specific places we want to visit. We even have a certain ability to influence others and create things. But, in all that, it is still limited power. However, God is not limited. He is *El Shaddai*—the all-powerful and all-sufficient One!

When we talk about God's omnipotence, it's not just a concept but a reality— and if so, worthy of our faith. Jesus put it this way: "For this reason the Father loves Me, because I lay down My life so that I may take it again. No one has taken it away from Me, but I lay it down on My own initiative. I have authority to lay it down, and I have authority to take it up again. This commandment I received from My Father."[2] In other words, He has the power and dominion over the most final aspect of life— death! And since He has absolute sovereignty, He is also the perfect provider for salvation and life.

Elijah learned about sovereignty and passed on his understanding to Elisha. One of the lessons surely involved a retelling of the nation of Israel's first encounter with the city of Jericho. Jericho was the third dojo stop visited by Elijah and Elisha. As it happened, Israel had heard of Jericho from the twelve spies, but this was the first time the children of Israel had laid their eyes upon this beautiful, fortified city. In the endgame, the walls of Jericho came tumbling down. It was a magnificent picture of the sovereignty of God exhibited for His people.

2 - Jn. 10:17-18

Jericho means *moon city*—fragrant place, to smell with pleasure, to delight in. The people of Jericho worshiped the moon goddess, which many theologians, in my theological studies, claimed to be the same demonic entity that is behind the empowerment of all false religions and cults. Jericho was also known as the *city of palm trees* (kind of like the beautiful city of San Diego where I live). And in the mind of the Jerichoites, it was well worth protecting. It was also considered to be impregnable. That sounds like the same kind of pride that those who built the *Titanic* walked in when they said that it couldn't sink.

The Lord miraculously led Israel across the Jordan River on dry ground. Everyone from the surrounding areas heard of it, and their hearts melted with fear— including those in the city of Jericho. Jericho's fear was somewhat abated because their city was supposed to be impenetrable. The next step though wasn't so much miraculous as it was painful. God had them stop in Gilgal and had all the men circumcised because they were going to have to go to war to claim the Promised Land. And they could not go to war for God if they were not in covenant with Him—ouch!

When they finally healed up from their latest physical and mental scarring episode, their first assignment was to take down this fortress of a city.[3] These walls were humongous; large enough to house people! I've heard it said that the walls of Jericho were so big that chariot races were held atop the walls for entertainment. Whether that's a teacher's imagination emerging or reality, it reveals the enormity of the situation

3 - Josh. 6:1-21

the Israelites faced.

The Lord had an interesting approach for Israel to overcome Jericho. Some major points should be noted in the sixth chapter of the book of Joshua:

- God said He was giving Israel the city along with their king and its valiant warriors.

- All the men marched around the city once a day for six days and were instructed to not say a word until Joshua said so. Seven priests carried rams' horns before the ark of God during the seven days to blow at the appropriate time.

- On the seventh day, they walked around the city seven times and then the priests blew the rams' horns.

- When the people heard the horns blow, Joshua told them to "Shout! For the Lord has given you the city...!"[4]

- The walls of Jericho came tumbling down.

- The Israelites went straight ahead and captured the city.

The Mindset of the Jericohites

Thousands of the inhabitants of Jericho during those seven days were probably standing on those massive walls looking down and saying, "How ridiculous those people look down there walking around our city with a

4 - Josh. 6:16

li'l box and some trumpets. If you're gonna play us a tune, get on with it already! Those Israelites must not like each other too much 'cuz they haven't said a single word to each other this whole time." And we all know that if you or I had been marching around those walls for seven days, we would have wanted to give everyone around us a piece of our mind. And not just a small piece, but a super-sized chunk—just grumbling and complaining the day and night away.

Grumbling and complaining are sins to God. Someone self-absorbed can't possibly be constantly alert and sober to the spirit of God. Grumbling and complaining weakens our faith and hinders our effectiveness—not to mention—diminishes our witness. We talk ourselves out of victory and right into defeat. To be one who doesn't grumble and complain, you have to be acutely aware that He is living in you. If you are busy murmuring, you are not busy believing. Could that be why God commanded His people to be silent?

If you don't believe in the sovereignty of God, you're doomed to impart doubt and unbelief into your disciples instead of faith and hope. One of my favorite passages addressing this concept says:

Who is among you that fears the LORD, that obeys the voice of His servant, that walks in darkness and has no light? Let him trust in the name of the LORD and rely on his God. Behold, all you who kindle a fire, who encircle yourselves with firebrands, walk in the light of your fire and among the brands you have set ablaze. This you will have from My hand: You will lie down in torment.[5]

   To trust in Him and rely on Him lies at the very foundation of our success as disciple-makers. And, the truth be told, it's no easy task to trust in and rely on anyone, let alone God. But it is only when we truly grasp the sovereignty of God and understand His provisions that we can travel to the fourth pit stop and confidently graduate to the red belt level of discipleship.

Cool Down Devotional Stretches:

As a little boy, I grew up loving Ohio State University and the University of Southern California. My father was from Akron, Ohio and was an avid lover of the OSU Buckeyes. There was nothing better than watching those two schools play each other on January 1st in the Rose Bowl. And, either way, I won! Lo and behold, my senior year of high school, I received a call from *The* Ohio State University about coming to play football! Can you say, "DREAM COME TRUE"?! But suddenly, due to unforeseen and uncontrollable events, it fell through just like that. I ended up at another not-so-football powerhouse, OSU (Oregon State University). In all honesty, the enthusiasm level dropped off a bit. But a couple years after leaving OSU I came to realize it was the best thing that ever happened to me. It is where I met AC Green, eventual member of the Los Angeles Lakers Showtime Crew and NBA Iron Man. It changed me spiritually and my walk with God for all eternity! The apostle Paul wrote, "And we know that God causes all things to work together for good to those who love God, to those who are called according to

5 - Isa. 50:10-11

His purpose."[6] God Himself got Job's attention regarding His sovereignty with this rhetorical question, "Where were you when I laid the foundation of the earth?"[7]

Alright, put your bookmark in and set the book aside for a while! Sovereignty is a big one! Time to be honest with yourself and examine the areas, situations, and circumstances in your life where, out of fear and mistrust, you tighten your grip instead of "letting go and letting God!" Find someone further along in their walk than you are and share with them the areas of your life where trust is hard to come by, where you can't see the way out or believe that God can make a way out?

Chapter 9

Approval

Chapter 9 - Red Belt: Approval

Certain seasons in our lives culminate with graduation to the next level. This particular event at the Jordan River was like graduation day for Elisha. And God seemed to be the proud papa, blessing Elisha with the keys to a car that had a super revved-up engine—a double portion if you will!

One of the things this particular story has taught me is that God is a kind, merciful God who desires us to understand that preparation precedes success. When we take into account that God knew beforehand that Elisha was going to ask for a *double portion* of what Elijah was carrying, we realize that the preparation had to be deep. These dojo stops were exactly that.

So, there they were at the final discipleship dojo stop, a place they had been many times before. But, this time it was different. Elijah was pretty clued in to what was about to happen and knew this was the final test for Elisha. By now, Elijah also knew Elisha wasn't going to leave his side until the end, but still went through the motions of asking Elisha to stay there while he went to the Jordan.[1] I wonder what Elijah could have been thinking in these last moments with his protégé. After six or more years of being together, they likely held a deep, brotherly love for one another that, I imagine, superseded the task of grooming Elisha to take his place as God's prophet. I

1 - 2 Kings 2:6-14

don't see Elijah as a very sappy person. But I can picture him and Elisha laughing, joking around, and talking about the things of God around a fire at night after a long day of training at the school of prophets. I can picture a friendship and covenant relationship for sure.

One day in eternity I want to look on the jumbo screen in heaven and see Elijah take his mantle and slap the Jordan River with it, seeing the river part as they cross over on dry land. Although it had happened with the Red Sea and the Jordan River before, I don't think it could ever get old to see. But what I really want to see is the intimate exchange that took place soon thereafter between Elijah and Elisha. Too often we can read the Word of God in such a sterile manner and without our imagination, especially if we have read the Word of God for years. But what happens at this point in the saga deserves our attention. I call this next interaction between Elijah and Elisha the *test of approval*, which I believe was an intimate time for both of them.

In this next scene between Elijah and Elisha, a very interesting foreshadowing takes place that points to an encounter Jesus had at the Jordan River with His Father and His cousin, John the Baptist. Jesus came to get baptized by John in the Jordan River. After Jesus came up out of the water, the Holy Spirit descended upon Him. "And then a voice came out of heaven, 'You are my beloved Son, in You I am well-pleased.'"[2] The Bible then proceeds to tell us that the Holy Spirit led Jesus into the wilderness to be tempted for forty days and nights, and upon completion of that temptation, Jesus returned in the power of the Holy Spirit.

2 - Lk. 3:22

Here, Elijah asks Elisha, "'Ask what I shall do for you before I am taken from you.' And Elisha said, 'Please, let a double portion of your spirit be upon me.' He said, 'You have asked a hard thing. Nevertheless, if you see me when I am taken from you, it shall be so for you; but if not, it shall not be so.'"[3]

The first time the mantle fell on Elisha he gave it back to Elijah. He understood the implications of it and decided that he was in no condition to bear the weight that accompanied the mantle of the prophet. Then, several years later, it fell upon Elisha again, but that time it was different. Now the landscape had changed. Maybe you can remember what it was like to go off to college or on your first solo flight from home, and the fear, the uncertainty, and the unknown you encountered blended together with excitement for the future. Now the future has arrived, and it's time for graduation. Things have changed, but many have stayed the same. Graduation is always exciting, but also carries with it the sobriety of having to cut your teeth and make your own way.

There you stand, on the precipice of your future, wondering if you have what it takes to move forward. Have you learned all that you needed to from your mentor? Will this work for you as it did for your discipler? You find yourself calling out in your heart as Elisha did, "Where is the God of Elijah?" Then you take your first step alone and find out that the same approval Elijah had from God is now on you.

There are seasons when you have to walk into your destiny alone. There's a reticence about the

3 - 2 Kgs. 2:9-10

unknown and the natural mourning of no longer having that person you always leaned on there. The process of commissioning and anointing is no small jaunt. It can be an intense boot camp. But, if embraced, there is the promise of a powerful manifestation of God's purposes in our lives. It also creates the opportunity to lead others into a similar experience—just as Elisha followed Elijah and had a school of prophets waiting for him on the other side of the Jordan.

There's no doubt that God wants us to reproduce in others the same thing that was reproduced in Elisha through his relationship with Elijah. But are you willing to go through the process of commissioning and anointing? That word *anointing* isn't just something given to you, but something smeared and rubbed into the very fiber of your being and, in turn, naturally experienced through the nature of who you are.

Many times Elijah said to Elisha, "Please stay here!" In true discipleship, there is no begging the pupil to follow, no chasing after him or her, just a definitive choice that has to be made. Elisha's heart expression was, "I will not leave you as long as you live!" Simply put, his heart was functioning from a covenant disposition.

Make no mistake about it. There's a cost to be counted and a price to be paid. And if you count the cost and pay the price, there's a mantle to be worn and an anointing to be had. By maneuvering through these four discipleship dojo stops, you are all but guaranteed to become a select arrow in God's quiver to be released at the appropriate time. Graduating from these four dojo stops leads you to the black belt level of discipleship.

Cool Down Devotional Stretches:

Rejection is a hard thing to deal with. I can't even imagine what the most rejected being to ever exist, Lucifer, feels like—his choices got him cast out of God's presence like lightning! Lord knows I've had my share of knockdown, drag-out battles with rejection stemming from parents getting divorced, unfair politics in most levels of my football career, and my eventual wife initially kicking-me-to-the-curb before coming to her senses a few years later (LOL)! In the mid-nineties, I was steeped in campus ministry which involved reaching out to university students daily. Every day that I went to campus, the battle raged on to conquer the fear of rejection! Then, one fateful day, on my way to campus, my Heavenly Father clearly spoke to me saying, "You know...when my Son walked this earth, they had to deal with Him. He lives in you now—NOW THEY HAVE TO DEAL WITH YOU!" At that moment, a supernatural understanding of His approval, commissioning, and anointing in my life became crystal clear! The impending fear I faced daily quickly began to diminish. Your Heavenly Father wants to cause fear to be destroyed in your life as well!

Do me a favor, dog-ear the corner of the book, shut it, close your eyes, and think deeply about this next question. Do you understand the covenantal, inherited approval afforded you due to the shedding of Jesus' blood for your salvation? If you struggle with feeling approved by God, ask the Holy Spirit to reveal to you the lies and/or condemnation the enemy is attacking you with. Then partner with someone to help you overcome this battle!

Chapter 10

Reproduction

Chapter 10 - Black Belt: Reproduction

The illustrious Oswald Chambers, in one of the most famous daily devotionals ever written, *My Utmost for His Highest*, said, "The great essential of the missionary is that he remains true to the call of God, and realizes that his one purpose is to disciple men and women to Jesus."[v] While speaking with His most devoted disciples right before ascending into heaven, Jesus expressed what seemed to be the most important thing on His heart:

> *And Jesus came up and spoke to them, saying, 'Go therefore and make disciples of all the nations (ethnos/ethnicities), baptizing them in the name of the Father and the Son and the Holy Spirit, teaching them to observe all that I commanded you; and lo, I am with you always, even to the end of the age.'*[1]

Many would call that evangelism. Though there is an aspect of evangelism to that command, it wasn't a command to evangelize. It wasn't a command to go plant churches and then make disciples, either. It was to make disciples and then plant churches from that growth (I'm just sayin'!). His command was to engage this world and immerse it into His character and nature, teach others to observe *all* that He commanded, and understand that He

1 - Mt. 28:18-20

was sending the Holy Spirit to us so that we would never be alone. That is a far cry from what the church looks like today.

We have an observation problem and desperately need to hone this particular skill. He didn't say to acknowledge all that He has commanded, but to observe. The Greek word for *observe* is the word *tēreō*. It means to keep, observe; to keep watch over, guard; to hold, reserve, preserve; to fulfill, pay attention to, keep on, or obey.[vi] These words describe something much weightier than the notion of just simply acknowledging and agreeing with something communicated to us.

I so clearly remember my journey of becoming a disciple and coming to realize that *observing all that He has commanded* was the map used to fulfill that destiny. I recall that pivotal day when I felt the prompting of the Holy Spirit leading me to get up and walk down the isle of Shiloh Baptist Church in Denver, Colorado to profess my love for Jesus and give my heart to Him. It was the longest walk of my life. It seemed as if the aisle kept getting longer and longer, but finally, I made it to one of the many seats aligned at the front of the altar. These seats had been put there for those who would make the most important decision of their lives—to receive Jesus as Lord.

I was third in line as the pastor made his way down the seats asking each person to describe why they came down front and what had taken place in their hearts. There I was, this 12- or 13-year-old boy with a mic in his face, blurting out boldly, "I love the Lord and I want to serve Him with all of my heart!" I remember thinking after that, "Wow, where did that come from?" But the next

14 years or so didn't quite parallel that bold declaration. Don't get me wrong. I was always considered a nice, sweet kid who didn't get into trouble, described by all as a good person. But I was not serving Him with all of my heart by any stretch of the imagination. In all those years since being *born again*, I never received instruction on how to follow Him, how to serve Him. I didn't even know where to begin!

The church I grew up in was full of wonderful hearts who loved the Lord. They just didn't have a strong revelation about discipleship (sound familiar?). The Bible tells us that "A slave will not be instructed by words alone; For though he understands, there will be no response."[2]

As human beings, though we get *born again*, we still have our flesh and past life to contend with; and therefore we must be instructed on how to walk in the ways of God and leave behind the ways of the world. There's no *red pill* to take, no *Genie's lamp* to rub; *Dorothy's red shoes* aren't hiding in the closet ready to click. There's just good old-fashioned faith in God, coupled with instruction and observation. That's what took place in my life in 1992. I got introduced to spiritual instruction, observation, commitment, and true devotion that is often simply called *discipleship*.

I distinctly recall the moment my eyes were opened, when I realized I wasn't a disciple and that I needed to change. The year before I moved to Los Angeles from Oregon had been one marked by a spiritual crisis. I later understood that God was getting my attention, looking to cash in on His investment that had taken place

2 - Pr. 29:19

in me years earlier.

The God of the spiritual reroutes orchestrated a reconnection with a college classmate of mine named AC Green. At the time, he was playing for the Los Angeles Lakers and had been an integral part of what was affectionately known as *Showtime* back in the '80s and early '90s. God used him as an essential ingredient of the remedy for my spiritual crisis. I had such a respect for the way AC had lived his life in college that God knew the kind of sway he would have in my life. During this time, I joined the church AC attended and immersed myself in the culture that permeated that particular church family. I encountered many people living as AC did. I saw a different lifestyle in effect. I began to hear this term *disciple* referenced much more than the term *Christian*. I didn't even hear people referring to themselves as Christians as much as I heard them calling themselves disciples.

I'll never forget the day I came across this particular passage of scripture in the book of Acts:

The news about them reached the ears of the church at Jerusalem, and they sent Barnabas off to Antioch. Then when he arrived and witnessed the grace of God, he rejoiced and began to encourage them all with resolute heart to remain true to the Lord; for he was a good man, and full of the Holy Spirit and of faith. And considerable numbers were brought to the Lord. And he left for Tarsus to look for Saul; and when he had found him, he brought him to Antioch.

Black Belt: Reproduction

And for an entire year they met with the church and taught considerable numbers; and the disciples were first called Christians in Antioch.[3]

Wait a second! What was that? They were first called Christians in Antioch? What? You mean that term wasn't first coined in Jerusalem where everything went down with Christ? And it wasn't the followers of Jesus Christ who coined the term "Christian"? It was the unbelievers? For me that was revolutionary, entirely eye-opening. I had spent 14 years or so calling myself a Christian when I wasn't one. I mean, how could I be? I hadn't become disciplined in the ways of Christ in all those years, so how could I actually be like Christ. The Christians didn't even call themselves Christians. They referred to themselves as believers, followers—*disciples*.

This was so convicting to me that I stopped calling myself a Christian. Besides, think about it—am I even truly qualified to declare to someone, "Hi! I'm Gino, and I'm like Christ"? I mean, wouldn't it be better if I simply lived in such a way that unbelievers could look at my life and say, "That guy's life resembles Christ's life!" as it was in the book of Acts?

What also struck me as crucial was that it said, "And they met for a year and considerable numbers were taught," indicating that during that year of teaching some obvious transformation had taken place through deep instruction and impartation. They were so changed that it caused the people of Antioch to come up with their own way of describing true disciples of Christ—Christians!

3 - Acts 11:22-26

Ever since then, I have encountered thousands of people who call themselves Christians but don't live in a way that their lives could confirm that as fact. I'm not saying that to be mean or sound judgmental. And I am not saying that they are not a part of His body, His family. If there was true repentance in their hearts then, of course, they are resting in His hands. Let's be clear, I'm not addressing the newborn infants and toddlers in Christ, but those who have been at this for a while without seeing the growth that "should" have taken place. There is a lack of maturity due to a lack of training. The self-declaration of being a Christian without actual manifested proof is one of the main reasons the world shuns the church and Christianity.

The world sees the majority of Christians as hypocrites (albeit, unintentional hypocrites). Nobody intentionally walks around in the body of Christ wanting to be a hypocrite. How ridiculous would that be! Have you ever heard of a newborn child proclaiming themselves a full grown adult? I think not. The words "disciple" and "Christian" are not simply a matter of semantics as many would have you believe...but one actually leads to the other!

When I was seven years old, my dad bought me my first football helmet, but that didn't make me a football player. I was on the football team, but it was the subsequent training I received over many years that made me a "football player" and allowed me to reach the highest level possible. That training gave me the opportunity, for a short period of time, to chase around Hall of Fame greats such as Joe Montana, Steve Young, and Warren Moon. But, without that training, I would have been snacking on the couch watching someone else do what I longed to do. I don't want you or me to be found snacking on the proverbial "spiritual couch." I want you and me in the spiritual game that God has ordained us to be in – defeating the adversary!

When there is a lack of training it naturally leads us to carelessness, apathy, hardness of heart, and habitual sinning, which, in turn, leads us to bondage and oppression by the enemy. This kind of training provides the needed "antihistamine" of inner-healing and deliverance in our souls which helps combat the schemes of the devil to bind us up and oppress those who follow Jesus. An acronym I love to use for sin is—S. I. N., Sitting In Neutral. I want this book to provoke you out of sin if that's where you find yourself. Not just the sin of commission but the sin of omission as well. James, the brother of Jesus, tells us, "Therefore, to the one who knows the right thing to do and does not do it, to him it is sin!" I love you too much to allow neutral to be the gear you find yourself sitting in. One of the few places neutral works is in our cars. But, in life, neutral is a fallacy; we are either moving forward or rolling backwards—let's not deceive ourselves!

For years, I've heard people say, as I have, "You should gather twelve men as Jesus did and disciple them because He's our model and example to follow." Well, over the years, my perspective has changed a bit because those twelve were specifically designated to be apostles. He is not calling all of us to be apostles. But He is calling all of us to be discples and disciple-makers! Jesus is absolutely the model and should be emulated to the best of our ability through the directing of the Holy Spirit. But, no matter how seasoned I am at this discipleship "thang," I definitely wouldn't claim to have Jesus' chops. But, oh, I pray one day!

For those of us who aren't Jesus, I find that the Apostle Paul, being the hall of fame spiritual coach that he was, implemented a great coaching game plan. He said, "The things which you have heard from me in the presence of many witnesses, entrust these to faithful men who will be able to teach others also."[4]

I believe Paul probably felt like this was a foolproof way for Timothy to preserve the *heirloom seed* of discipleship that Paul had deposited into him without becoming overwhelmed by the task. I say *heirloom seed* because that's what Paul received on the backside of the Arabian desert, as he was appointed by Jesus with the mission of being the Apostle to the Gentiles:

> *And when we had all fallen to the ground, I heard a voice saying to me in the Hebrew dialect, "Saul, Saul, why are you persecuting Me? It is hard for you to kick against the goads." And I said, "Who are You, Lord?" And the Lord said, "I am Jesus whom you are persecuting. But get up and stand on your feet; for this purpose I have appeared to you, to appoint you a minister and a witness not only to the things which you have seen, but also to the things in which I will appear to you; rescuing you from the Jewish people and from the Gentiles, to whom I am sending you, to open their eyes so that they*

4 - 2 Tim. 2:2

> *may turn from darkness to light and from the*
> *dominion of Satan to God, that they may receive*
> *forgiveness of sins and an inheritance among*
> *those who have been sanctified by faith in Me."*
> *So, King Agrippa, I did not prove disobedient to*
> *the heavenly vision, but kept declaring both to*
> *those of Damascus first, and also at Jerusalem*
> *and then throughout all the region of Judea, and*
> *even to the Gentiles, that they should repent and*
> *turn to God, performing deeds appropriate to*
> *repentance.*[5]

I have found that the discipleship process across many churches in the body of Christ is a GMO version of discipleship. There is a lot of classwork, memorization, and reading of books, but very little true impartation of the nature of a true disciple-maker. We get seduced into unconsciously believing that discipleship is about the dissemination of information. And why wouldn't we? Knowledge is at our fingertips and comes to us at the speed of light. There is a prevailing hurried spirit in the body of Christ when it comes to preparing people for the task of fulfilling the *Great Commission (because people want to "rush" Jesus back to get us and go to Heaven)*. But I don't see in the Bible where Jesus, Paul, or the other disciples rushed their disciples to grow.

I will remind us of what my dear friend, Lakita Wright, stated in her endorsement of this book, "Christ instructed His soon-to-be apostles, very much like a sensei runs a dojo: I do, you watch; you do, I correct, and repeat. This "way" of training, or transformation, is antithetical to our Western understanding of teaching;

5 - Acts 26:14-20

you talk, I take notes, ask questions, and take a quiz." I was an avid player of multiple sports starting at age seven and I had many coaches. I found that there was a great deal more on-field instruction than there was meeting-room teaching going on. More is relationally caught than taught—I can teach you till I'm blue in the face, but who I am is what I will impart. Remember, discipleship is relationship!

Paul was very much about making sure people got the *heirloom seed* of discipleship. His admonition to Timothy proved so when he gave what has been described as the *Four Generational Transference*: "The things which you [Timothy-2nd generation] have heard from me [Paul-1st generation] in the presence of many witnesses, entrust these to faithful men (*and women*) [3rd generation] who will be able to teach others [4th generation] also."[6] So, Paul taught Timothy, who was to teach faithful men and women who could then teach others. There will always be many witnesses. But it's those who understand lordship and the process of heirloom seed transformation that become the faithful ones we can teach and impart the *heirloom seed* of discipleship—and, eventually, can make those who receive the heirloom seed into disciple-makers.

Much like a parent and child relationship, the discipleship relationship needs to stay true and strong to remain fruitful—each person growing consistently and being transformed into the glorious image of Jesus more and more. It ain't easy. Jesus said, "You have to eat my flesh and drink my blood!"[7] It doesn't sound that delectable, but,

6 - 2 Tim.2:2 (notes mine)
7 - Jn. 6:56

deep within the spirit of a person, it's more than satisfying once digested. It's a safe bet to assume Peter was not overjoyed to hear that eating of flesh and drinking of blood was required—and who would be? (Of course, Jesus was speaking figuratively, describing the to-come remembrance of Him through communion.) But in the depths of his soul Peter knew Jesus had the words of life and realized that if he was ever to become like His Lord and Savior, this was par for the course. *Bon appétit!*

  This is what was required of those who walked with Jesus, those who were taught by the original apostles, and those who followed Paul. And, I believe this is what is required now for anyone who claims the name of Jesus, our Lord and Savior. Through the process of becoming disciple-makers, we embrace our Lord's sovereign authority given to Him by the Father of heaven and earth.

Cool Down Devotional Stretches:

Knowledge imparted is much more impactful than knowledge that is simply disseminated. Knowledge imparted is much more taxing than knowledge merely shared. It is human nature for human beings to mentally ascend to knowledge acquired only to fail when the rubber meets the road. We fail because we do not truly own the acquired knowledge we "thought" we possessed. From age 11-14 I spent my summers on the campus of Prairie View A & M University. I absolutely love basketball as much as football and was blessed to have been adopted by the university basketball team my first summer there. As it would happen, they had the SWAC scoring champ on their team--a sharp-shooting marksman from outside named Larry Hagan, and it just so happened, that he took to me! Larry spent my first summer there instructing me how to shoot properly. Not telling me, but imparting into me the mechanics and nature of a shooter. He would constantly say to me, "Look here lil' bruh, a pure shooter can hit 9 out of 10 shots consistently; a consistent shooter can hit 7 to 8 out of 10 shots consistently. I didn't quite reach "pure shooter" status, but at my peak I was definitely a "consistent shooter" due to all that Larry imparted into me as well as the discipline of practice that he also instilled into me. You are what you practice, good or bad! John, the beloved said, "Little children, make sure no one deceives you; the one who practices righteousness is righteous, just as He is righteous; the one who practices sin is of the devil!"[8]

Time to test yourself. Jesus said, "By this My Father in heaven is glorified, that you bear much fruit and so prove to be My disciples."[9] What do you need to do, that you have not been doing, to prove that you are a fruit-bearing disciple of Jesus? Have you thought about what you might say on that day you're standing before the Father and He asks you, "Did you make any disciples of My Son while you were on earth?"

8 - 1 Jn. 3:7-8a (NASB)
9 - Jn. 15:8 (ESV)

Black Belt: Reproduction

Chapter 11

Spiritual Authority
in Discipleship

Chapter 11 – Spiritual Authority in Discipleship

I have heard it said that whenever someone is dying or leaving with the possibility that you might not see them again, you should listen closely to their parting words because you will find out from their heart what is most important to them. I believe that to be true with Jesus just before He ascended to heaven to sit at the right hand of the Father. He was setting things in order and giving what He knew to be the most important instructions to His followers assembled there.

Jesus immediately set the tone at the last gathering before He ascended to heaven by declaring, "All authority in heaven and on earth has been given to me...Go therefore and make disciples..."[1] He has made this same authority accessible to us not for our selfish, personal gain but to help fulfill the purposes of God, giving Him the glory. Oh, how the servant-leaders in the body of Christ have failed at times in understanding this revelation!

My lovely wife, Michelle, and I have discussed this subject in depth many times over. I believe you'll enjoy hearing some of her thoughts on the matter in the following pages.

What Is Spiritual Authority?

1 - Mt. 28:18

People were surprised by many of the teachings and actions of Jesus—such as walking on water. What? He healed a little girl whom everyone knew was dead. What? Then, just to be sure that everyone understood that He is Lord, He waited four days to raise one of His best friends from the dead. What??? Mind blown!

Yet, despite how incredible those miracles were, what we see in the Word that truly blew people away was His authority! When Jesus had finished speaking these words in the synagogue it says, "They were *amazed* at His teaching; for He was teaching them as one having *authority*, and not as their scribes."[2]

This authority didn't stop with Jesus. One day Peter and John were walking together to the temple for daily prayers. A man who had been lame from birth was begging and asked them for money; instead, Peter replied, "I do not possess silver and gold, but what I do have I give to you: 'In the name of Jesus Christ the Nazarene—walk!'"[3] Then the religious people began to run to them and were "filled with wonder and amazement."[4] Peter proceeded to tell them, in no uncertain terms, how they murdered the Messiah, which resulted in Peter and John's arrests (v. 15). Jesus' authority was passed on to His disciples.

One of the more powerful passages in the book of Acts tells us, "Now as they [the rulers and elders of the people] observed the confidence of Peter and John, and understood that they were uneducated and untrained men, they were *marveling*, and began

2 - Mk. 1:22
3 - Acts 3:6
4 - Acts 3:10

184

to recognize them as having been with Jesus."[5] Why? Because the authority given to them by Jesus was reflected in the confidence, boldness and wisdom displayed in their encounter with the elders. They were amazed and "marveling" at the authority with which they spoke. Jesus had been the only person like this they had seen before who moved in this kind of authority. It was obvious to all present that these men had been with Him. This is true spiritual authority.

Wow! Could I ever walk in that kind of authority? How do I get it? In the book of Acts, one man offered to buy it.[6] That did not go well for him. You can't buy it. You don't earn it. As we read above, it comes from having been with Jesus, having been discipled in His ways. One grows in spiritual authority by obeying Jesus. It is received by faith and is imparted to you by another who already possesses it— like Elijah to Elisha, Moses to Joshua, and Jesus to His disciples.

True authority, especially spiritual authority, has very little to do with a position or title. The Pharisees, Sadducees, and scribes had all the positions and titles, but they didn't have real authority. They had rules and power. Jesus had no position or status. Jesus was of *low birth*, regarded as a bastard by the world. The circumstances of Jesus' birth were a bit sketchy. Joseph and Mary were married suddenly and the baby came a little too soon after this shotgun wedding for people not to be skeptical of their pre-marital interactions. In our modern culture, couples

5 - Acts 4:13
6 - Acts 8:1-2

have babies without being married all the time. It has become very common, even in vogue. However, in Jesus' day, giving birth to an illegitimate child resulted in tremendous shame for the child and the entire family. Yet, in reality, He was the Son of God, the Prince of Peace and the rightful, sovereign King of the nation of Israel.

He was a carpenter, a blue-collar, working-class man. One commentary suggests that He was a builder or laborer. In our modern context, I imagine something like a construction worker or furniture maker. Regardless of His exact job description, He did manual labor. Though I have no doubt that Jesus, in human terms, was mind-blowingly intelligent, the Bible does not speak of Him having any formal higher education or degree to show for it. While any honest labor is certainly respectable, according to the moors of the day, Jesus was a commoner or a peasant— a "regular Joe." "He had no beauty or majesty to attract us to Him, nothing in His appearance that we should desire Him."[7] Yet, in reality, He was the co-Creator and Chief Architect of all things and all people.[8]

He was a Jew who lived under the occupation and domination of a foreign, conquering people. Every kid in America has probably uttered, "You can't make me do it. It's a free country." Well, that was not the case for Jesus (or anyone else in Israel for that matter). He grew up powerless and in subjection to Roman rulers and godless authorities who could demand service of subjects at their whim, hence Jesus' *extra*

7 - Isaiah 53:2
8 - Jn. 1:3

mile statement: "Whoever forces you to go one mile, go with him two."[9] It was legal and customary for a Roman soldier to force any subject to carry his supplies for up to one mile at any time.[vii] One had to comply or face harsh repercussions. Jesus was treated as a common Jew at the time, poorly and with disrespect. Yet, in reality, He was the King of kings and the government would rest on His shoulders![10]

People called Jesus *Rabbi*, which means *teacher*, but we don't see anything in the Bible to suggest that He had a synagogue or any official duties in the temple that He was overseeing. However, He often functioned within the system as well as outside of it. Jesus went to Jerusalem for the festivals. He told the people to do as the Pharisees and experts said, but not to do as they do. He simultaneously taught them in streets, fields, and homes the deeper and more foundational things of God. He was leading them into true worship of the Father in direct contrast to the religious leaders' teachings.

In the Word's first account, where we see Jesus speaking truth to people in the synagogue, the people were loving it and "wondering at the gracious words that were falling from His lips..."[11] But, only a few minutes later, He got too real for them. "And ALL the people in the synagogue were filled with rage as they heard these things; and they got up and drove Him out of the city, and led Him to the brow of the hill on which their city had been built, in order to throw Him down

9 - Mt. 5:41
10 - Isa. 9:6
11 - Lk. 4:22

the cliff."[12] They tried to kick the rebel and dissenter out and put an end to Him. Yet, in reality He was and is God, the second person of the Trinity, and He is the true temple—the embodiment of what they were supposed to be worshiping.[13]

From the time Jesus left His family home and began His ministry at the age of 30, He was effectively homeless. He followed the leading of the Holy Spirit and moved from area to area. "A scribe came and said to Him, 'Teacher, I will follow You wherever You go.' Jesus said to him, 'The foxes have holes and the birds of the air have nests, but the Son of Man has nowhere to lay His head'"[14] Yet, "the earth is the Lord's and everything in it."[15] Jesus was asking this scribe to count the costs of following Him.

Some people are commitment phobes, but others will eagerly commit to all kinds of requests only to flake out later. Even if they do fulfill their commitment, likely it's pretty lacking in joy, emerging more from a sense of duty. This pattern, left unchecked, will lead to burnout and dead religion.

Furthermore, when Jesus says, "the Son of Man has nowhere to lay His head..." that word *head* is symbolic of His authority. God, the Father, is commonly referred to as the *Godhead* in the Trinity. Jesus is the head of the church and He wants to rest His authority – His head – upon us,

12 - Lk. 4:28-29
13 - Mt. 26:61
14 - Mt. 8:19
15 - Ps. 24:1 (NLT)

His *body*.[16] However, we must make a whole-hearted commitment, which means we must understand what we're committing ourselves to and be mentally prepared and willing to pay that price. When we surrender ourselves fully to Him and His purposes — "not my will, but Yours be done"[17] — no matter the cost, we become dangerous, like a katana sword in the hands of Jesus.

I'm going on and on about Jesus' humiliations because this is one of the biggest reasons why He exuded such awe-inspiring authority. He walked in incredible authority, not because people knew He was Messiah—most of them didn't—but because *He* knew that He was Messiah. *He* knew that He was the Son of God, whether one single other person on the earth recognized it or not—including His own mama! His Father loved Him and was "well pleased" with Him.[18]

Jesus knew who He was so deep down inside of Himself that nothing and no one could shake Him or get Him to move in fear or insecurity. He had nothing to prove to anyone. Jesus, in all of His humanity, was so secure in the Father's love because He had developed a lifestyle of spending time alone with Him. "For we do not have a high priest who cannot sympathize with our weaknesses, but One who has been tempted in *all* things *just as we are*, yet without sin."[19] One of the ways that we are tempted is to believe that we are less (which creates fear and insecurity) or more (resulting in pride and selfishness) than God

16 - Eph. 1:22-23, 1 Cor. 11:3, Col. 1:18

17 - Luke 22:42

18 - Mk. 1:11 (NASB)

19 - Heb. 4:15

says we are.

The mind-boggling authority that Jesus walked in was because He was secure in His identity. His identity wasn't found in His gender as a man. Or, in His race as a Jew. It wasn't found in His career status as a carpenter or His religious role as a minister. It surely wasn't found in His reputation through the fickle things others said about Him.—"...they say, 'Behold a glutton and a drunkard, a friend of tax collectors and sinners!'"[20] Many, if not most people, were continually offended by Him and constantly talked badly about Him behind His back and to His face. Yet, His confidence in who He was never wavered.

But, how did He become so secure in His identity? He was just different from me because He was God, right? He *was* God, but He was God in the *flesh*—a mystery wrapped up in an enigma—the flesh is full of want and desire and insecurity. Jesus had to wrestle with his own fleshly nature just like we do. He didn't want to go to the cross. He asked the Father three times to be released from that end: "...take this cup away."[21] Jesus struggled so much under the strain and pressure of His impending course that He sweat blood. His identity was in being God's Son. The Father was well-pleased with His Son because Jesus sought after His Father and remained aligned with the Father at all times.[22] He walked in the character and nature of the Father and always obeyed the Father regardless of the external pressures: "...whatever the Father does,

20 - Mt. 11:19
21 - Mt. 26:39
22 - Lk. 2:49

these things the Son also does in like manner."[23] Jesus was discipled by His Father!

Jesus' identity was firmly rooted in His deep and abiding relationship with His Father. He spent time with His Father. He continually drew away to pray—to get alone with His Father. He needed the Father's presence, voice, guidance, and leading. It would help Him handle the craziness of the crowds. He didn't just spend time with God in the temple. That's what we try to do—live six days on our own and then check in once a week. That will leave us in a world of hurt, easily exploited and without much, or any, authority. Jesus spent time with the Father and surrounded Himself with the Father's peace, love, and affirmation. It was a continual cleansing as He walked throughout this dirty world.[24]

To quote Hans and Franz from *Saturday Night Live* back in the 80s, "Listen to me now and believe me later." If you have any insecurities, and you do—we all do—the devil will come to you in your weakest moment to tempt you, whether through pride, lust, attacks of sickness, or the promise of power, riches, and security. If you can be exploited, you will be. The problem is that some of his moves are so subtle and seem to line up with the Word. We can veer off course a tiny bit and never even know it until we've gone years down the road in the wrong direction. Do I really know Him? Do I really know who I am in Him?

Most of the time in the church, I hear the term

23 - Jn. 5:19
24 - Jn. 13:5-10

spiritual authority used to refer to a pastor or leader. For example, "I am under Pastor Bob's spiritual authority," or "So and so has spiritual authority over me." There are a few problems with this idea. First of all, what people are referring to is *positional authority.* There is a certain hierarchy in place where some people are over or under others with respect to position.

Hierarchies are not inherently bad and are even necessary, to an extent. However, we want to be careful of the *yeast of the Pharisees.* We are all fallen people, and position and power are very alluring and all too intoxicating. We all have basic human needs for affirmation and respect. We all also have very real insecurities. It is more than easy for us to move in what I call a "positional authority mindset." When we begin to think this way, we give too much respect to positions and titles. In the church, leaders may promote giftedness over character and then pay the price when that charismatic person's lack of character bites them in the rear later. The congregation may put pastors on a pedestal beyond their ability to sustain a particular image. When the pastors fail to meet overly high expectations, members can easily become judgmental or disillusioned with what they thought church was supposed to be like: "For we all stumble in many ways."[25]

I was saved as a college student at the University of Southern California in 1989 at the end of my Junior year. I was a hard-partying sorority girl who got radically saved and baptized in the Holy

25 - Jas. 3:2

Spirit. It was awesome! I have two distinct college experiences, my B.C. days and my A.D. days.

After I got saved (A.D. days), I was given a book to read entitled—you guessed it—*Spiritual Authority*. It is full of good biblical insights as to how one should relate to those in positions of authority. However, the deep impression I walked away with was an overarching fear of speaking against those in positions of authority. Ultimately, the spirit of the book even clouded my ability to see leaders and their flawed humanity clearly.

After almost 30 years in ministry, and in light of everything we see about Jesus and His authority, I now believe that that book should be entitled *Positional Authority*. When we become too concerned about speaking honestly to those who are in positions of authority, or there are consequences when we do dare to, an environment of control reveals itself, which stifles the growth of individuals and the church as a whole. As I have matured in the Lord, life, and ministry, I have become more aware of these tendencies of leaders (including myself) towards controlling others in the church.

Tasked with the challenge of making disciples, we can never allow ourselves to fall into a positional authority mindset. Leaders in the Bible are often referred to as *overseers*. However, God's Word gives us pretty severe warnings. He is much more concerned with abuse of His authority than with those daring upstarts who might challenge our little positions that we've carved out for ourselves: "Let not many of you become teachers, my brethren, knowing that you will incur a stricter judgment!"[26] Jesus said to His disciples:

> The kings of the Gentiles lord it over them; and those who have authority over them are called "Benefactors." But it is not this way with you, but the one who is the greatest among you must become like the youngest, and the leader like the servant. For who is greater, the one who reclines at the table or the one who serves? Is it not the one who reclines at the table? But I am among you as the one who serves.[27]

When the Lord uses the word woe, He is really serious, like Jonathan Edwards' falling into "the hands of an angry God" serious.[viii] Let's look at what Jesus has to say about the abuse of positional authority:

> Son of man, prophesy against the shepherds of Israel. Prophesy and say to those shepherds, 'Thus says the Lord GOD, "Woe, shepherds of Israel who have been feeding themselves! Should not the shepherds feed the flock?"'...but with force and severity you have dominated them.[28]

> 'Woe to the shepherds who are destroying and scattering the sheep of My pasture!' declares the

26 - Jas. 3:1
27 - Lk. 22:25-27
28 - Ezek. 34:2-4

LORD.[29]

Woe to the worthless shepherd who leaves the flock! A sword will be on his arm and on his right eye! His arm will be totally withered and his right eye will be blind.[30]

We must always operate under the fear of the Lord as we endeavor to represent Jesus. You may be thinking, "Is this really all that serious? I don't want to be a shepherd or pastor. I'm just learning how to be a disciple and how to disciple someone else." Yeah, you have a good point. There is so much extra grace for the young person who's growing in the basics of this walk with God, but as we grow older, wiser, and more educated in the Word, carrying more weight and responsibilities in life, our freedoms and room for error increasingly narrow: "...to whom much is given, from him much is required..."[31]

For someone embarking upon the journey of intentionally making disciples (which should be everyone who claims the name of the Lord), it is important to understand that being someone's discipler does not make you superior to them or give you a position over them. You are someone who has walked a little farther down the road in your spiritual walk than another. Now you can offer all that God has done in you—sharing your struggles, victories, defeats, and all that you've learned from them. That's

29 - Jer. 23:1
30 - Zech. 11:17
31 - Lk. 12:48 (NKJV)

where your true authority comes from, your life experiences and expertise. You have the chance to say, "Watch out for that pothole!" or "This hill is tough, but you can make it to the top—and the view is awesome!"

In discipleship, or any kind of ministry, we always want to be directing people toward Jesus rather than to ourselves. It's easy for a new believer to become very attached to their discipler. This is good and normal. However, they are not our disciples first. They are primarily Jesus' disciples. We want to give people all of the time and attention that they need, but we don't want them to become overly dependent on us, and we should also be very careful not to become intoxicated by their dependency. They should be able to make decisions for themselves. We should give them godly wisdom and point them to the Bible. Encourage them to seek wisdom from other solid believers besides us. Whether it's who to date, what job to take, a moral struggle, or another issue, "there is wisdom in a multitude of counselors."[32]

We will no doubt have our convictions about all sorts of things—and may share them based on the Word—but, understand that others may not share our viewpoints. For instance, my husband and I choose not to drink alcohol for several reasons, but most of my believing friends do not hold that conviction. I will explain to people why we don't drink if it comes up, but I don't try to push it upon them or guilt them into making the same life choices that I have made.

On another note, when talking to my kids

32 - Pr. 24:6 (NASB)

about their siblings, I say all the time, "You're not their parent. Stop bossing them. You appeal to them. Instead of yelling, 'Stop!' say, 'Would you please stop kicking my seat?'" One is an order; the other is an appeal. We're not just talking semantics. It's about our attitude.

A young disciple might just do whatever we tell them to do, particularly if they have trouble separating pleasing us from pleasing God. However, just like I tell my kids, we have no authority over them. We are not over others. As disciple-makers, we are out in front of them.

The Bible is our ultimate source of authority. We should remind people of what God has said. As Paul often said, "Spend time with Jesus in His Word and "pray at all times in the Spirit."[33] The more intimate we become with Jesus, the more of His true authority we will walk in. The more we humble ourselves before the Lord, the more we will become like Him and the more we will walk in our true identity, divine purpose, and genuine authority.

I have friends who have walked away from God because they have experienced a devastating blow of disappointment in a leader or leaders and the organization that they were a part of. During all of our time in ministry, my husband and I have experienced the good, the bad, and the ugly. We have even been betrayed by leaders we trusted, but we never wavered in our faith in God because, by the grace of God through discipleship, we had developed a lifestyle of relying on Jesus and had built a solid relationship

33 - Eph. 6:18

with Him even more foundational and real than our relationships with people.

The same imperfect, flawed people who hurt us, or merely let us down in big ways, are also the people who years earlier sacrificed much to make us into disciples of Jesus. They taught us to read the Bible daily for ourselves. They taught us to pray, deny ourselves, and submit to the Lordship of Jesus. They taught us to walk after Him with our whole hearts. They instilled in us godly convictions and imparted the passion for Jesus that ultimately sustained us when we were let down by their weaknesses and failings. They were imperfect people who gave us much, and we are forever indebted and grateful. And now we have also learned from their mistakes.

Spiritual authority requires a healthy relationship with God as well as knowing your identity and purpose in life. Jesus moved in such great authority because He truly and deeply knew His Father, who He was, and what He was supposed to do. Jesus was born to die: "The Spirit of the Lord is upon Me, because he anointed Me to preach the gospel to the poor. He has sent Me to proclaim release to the captives, and recovery of sight to the blind, to set free those who are oppressed, to proclaim the favorable year of the Lord."[34] And then He was to die for the sins of the world.[35]

He invites us into His purpose. If you want to be His disciple, pick up your cross daily and follow after

34 - Lk. 4:18-19
35 - 1 Cor. 15:3; 1 Tim. 1:15; Jn. 3:16

Him[36]:

> *For you have been called for this purpose,*
> *since Christ also suffered for you, leaving you*
> *an example for you to follow in His steps, who*
> *committed no sin, nor was any deceit found in*
> *His mouth; and while being reviled, He did not*
> *revile in return; while suffering, He uttered no*
> *threats, but kept entrusting Himself to Him who*
> *judges righteously; and He Himself bore our sins*
> *in His body on the cross, so that we might die to*
> *sin and live to righteousness; for by His wounds*
> *you were healed.*[37]

A person who knows Daddy, their identity and their purpose is dangerous in the kingdom of God— they're a disciple. Better yet, they become a disciple-maker!

Now, Gino and I are firmly established as a father and a mother, not just because of our age and natural kids, but because of our mentality. "For if you were to have countless tutors in Christ, yet you would not have many fathers; for in Christ Jesus I became your father through the gospel. Therefore I exhort you, be imitators of me..."[38] Now fathers have natural, positional authority, but their true authority comes from how well they have built relationships with their children. We long to have many spiritual children and are dead set on advancing His kingdom and building His church by making disciple-makers, because that's

36 - Mt. 16:24
37 - 1 Pet. 2:21-24
38 - 1 Cor. 4:15-16

what He told us to do.

Well, that was my wife and her musings regarding spiritual authority—and great musings I might add! In a nutshell, we have to have some semblance of authority or no one is going to follow us, but it has to be a godly authority. If not, it will eventually be snuffed out, and then no one's the better for it.

The Disposition of Authority: Humility

Authority is a bona fide drug that has to be regulated or it can destroy us like any other drug. God conveyed this sentiment to Moses during the "burning bush" encounter. Moses held a staff in his hand that would later on come to represent authority in the hands of Moses while delivering the children of Israel out of Egypt.[39] God told Moses to lay the staff down. When he did, it turned into a snake. God then proceeded to tell Moses to pick it up by the tail, which most people would absolutely not do with a poisonous snake. I believe God was saying to Moses, "Be careful how you handle My authority, do so in the fear of the Lord; because if you don't, it'll whip around and bite you or maybe even destroy you!" I feel this was a significant moment of trust for Moses and an opportunity for him to gain some understanding of how God views authority. A snake charmer usually grabs a snake by the neck, not the tail. This rod was probably a shepherd's crook, a long staff with a curved head--the tool used to exercise authority and protection over a flock. But Moses needed to understand that exercising authority over a flock of mindless sheep or cattle is quite different than exercising authority over those created in God's image!

39 - Ex. 3:2-3 (ESV)

Spiritual Authority in Descipleship

I often reflect on Jesus' instructions to His disciples about how we should approach authority in comparison to how the Scribes and the Pharisees approached authority:

> *Then Jesus spoke to the crowds and to His disciples, saying: "The scribes and the Pharisees have seated themselves in the chair of Moses; therefore all that they tell you, do and observe, but do not do according to their deeds; for they say things and do not do them. They tie up heavy burdens and lay them on men's shoulders, but they themselves are unwilling to move them with so much as a finger. But they do all their deeds to be noticed by men; for they broaden their phylacteries and lengthen the tassels of their garments. They love the place of honor at banquets and the chief seats in the synagogues, and respectful greetings in the market places, and being called Rabbi by men. But do not be called Rabbi; for One is your Teacher, and you are all brothers. Do not call anyone on earth your father; for One is your Father, He who is in heaven. Do not be called leaders; for One is your Leader, that is, Christ. But the greatest among you shall be your servant. Whoever exalts himself shall be humbled; and whoever humbles himself shall be exalted."[40]*

The scribes and Pharisees loved these titles of position and honor so much that they became authority "drunkards" and their judgment was impaired; therefore,

40 - Mt. 23:1-12

they didn't treat people the right way. Jesus isn't saying that we can't be *called* any of those things. No, He's saying don't call *ourselves* those things! Instead, live in Him in such a way that those things will be earned naturally through our humility.

I'm constantly teaching people things regarding my Lord and Savior Jesus Christ. I've led people and have been referred to as a spiritual father for years now. Each time I am humbled by it and reminded by the Holy Spirit of the responsibility of it, especially since I'm well acquainted with my own warts (if you know what I mean). That's why the fear of the Lord comes in handy. Humility is paramount—humility, humility, humility. (I'm just sayin'!)

Over the years I've seen a common mistake made by many believers, especially those who are young in their faith. They equate discipling with having authority over the disciple. That's simply not true! This is what the Word has to say about being a disciple when prophetically referencing Jesus (the ultimate Disciple) in Isaiah:

> **The Lord GOD has given Me the tongue of disciples, that I may know how to sustain the weary one with a word. He awakens Me morning by morning; He awakens My ear to listen as a disciple. The Lord GOD has opened My ear; and I was not disobedient, nor did I turn back.** [41]

The tongue of disciples given wasn't for the purpose of exercising authority over others, but was given to sustain those who were weary until they could

41 - Isa. 50:4-5

become strong! Therefore, when Jesus said, "All authority has been given to Me, go therefore and make disciples of all the nations..."[42] He wasn't saying to go and exercise authority over others, but, instead, to go and exercise the authority He's given us to train others to become disciples...and ultimately disciple-makers!

What is the ultimate purpose of the authority given to certain people? So glad you asked! The Bible explains it this way in Ephesians:

And He gave some as apostles, and some as prophets, and some as evangelists, and some as pastors and teachers, for the equipping of the saints for the work of service, to the building up of the body of Christ; until we all attain to the unity of the faith, and of the knowledge of the Son of God, to a mature man, to the measure of the stature which belongs to the fullness of Christ.[43]

So, it appears that the main reason for the authority that Jesus delegates to "some" is to equip, build, and mature the body until it reaches "the measure of the stature which belongs to the fullness of Christ."

Because of the misunderstanding of authority, this 12-letter word, *discipleship*, has been through the wringer over the years—and rightly so at times—due to the abusive behaviors of what people have called "discipleship." In an effort to make the concept more receptive in the body of Christ, we've tried to substitute

42 - Mt. 28:19
43 - Eph. 4:11-13

softer, milder words, such as mentoring and coaching because we know at a heart level that Jesus has called us to this ever-important spiritual endeavor. And although terms like mentoring and coaching are intricately woven into the word, *discipleship*, they don't fully capture the spiritual depth of what Jesus meant when He said, "Go therefore and make" them (using the "D" word!). At the end of the day, authority is given to help us become servant leaders in order to train others.

Cool Down Devotional Stretches:

Authority is a fickle mistress and can be quite seductive and dangerous if not handled with the respect it deserves. One of the most painful things I have ever experienced in my life was the betrayal of a once-upon-a-time best friend and leader. When it all came to light, many of those involved wanted me to "hogtie and horsewhip" the person for what they had done to me! But I kept hearing in my spirit, "For judgment will be merciless to one who has shown no mercy; mercy triumphs over judgment."[44] When it comes to dealing with authority and leaders, I've always held the principle in my heart that David echoed while being hunted by king Saul, "But David said to Abishai, 'Do not destroy him, for who can stretch out his hand against the Lord's anointed and be without guilt?'"[45] This didn't mean I could not question this person who hurt me and inquire as to why he did the things he did to me. But it also did not mean that I had license to belittle and demean that person whom God had placed in a position of authority—I am to trust that God is on the throne and adjudicating things as He sees fit.

44 - Jas. 2:13 (NASB)
45 - 1 Sam. 26:9 (NASB)

Okay, hit the pause button. This may be the time to repent to God and (maybe) a certain person or persons you have undermined because you did not respect their leadership. I get it, sometimes people make it hard to respect them and their leadership style, but it is a terrain that we must learn to navigate. Take a good amount of time and examine how you view authority. Is it in line with God's heart regarding authority? What have you viewed as the most important aspects of authority (i.e., titles, power, production, character, etc.)? Do you view authority more principally or practically speaking, spiritually, or naturally?

Chapter 12

Second Nature

Chapter 12 – Second Nature

Instruction and training are keys to spiritual growth. Proverbs directs us to, "Keep hold of instruction; do not let go; guard her, for she is your life."[1] John Maxwell, in his book *The 5 Levels of Leadership*, describes those levels as being "position (rights)," "permission (relationships)," "production (results)," "people development (reproduction)," "pinnacle (respect)," with level 4, "people development (reproduction)," being the most important. That's because level 4 is where people are being trained and made into "something."[ix] Anytime something of any significance is made, it takes time and effort. Training involves failure, but the more you train the less you fail because your training matures you.

When I think about training, I often think about the military and the different positions held. I have had some friends and several members of my family who have served in the military. Some had specialized training and earned the sexy title Navy SEAL. The title General is pretty sexy too, but you don't see too many movies made about the 5-star general or admiral who sent the SEALs in to get the bad guy...No, the movies are usually about the SEALs, often called "operators," who went in and got the bad guys.

I make this point because I have found a running theme. Whether they were a private first class, a Navy

1 - Pr. 4:13 (ESV)

SEAL, or a 4 or 5-star general/admiral, they all had to go through boot camp and get fully trained before being called a "soldier." I see too often that we pastors, five-fold ministry "generals/admirals," if you will, long to send our soldiers out into the battlefield so we can have them come back and give an awe-inspiring testimony (our version of a Navy SEAL movie). This is done to encourage and motivate others to join the army and make a difference.

The only problem is, spiritually speaking, many times people don't come back triumphant because they haven't been fully trained as a spiritual soldier (disciple). Many of them have not stepped into the discipleship dojo, or they were in the dojo and chose not to remain. Therefore, they linger somewhere in the "white belt to blue belt" stages and desperately need to move on through to the "purple belt to black belt" stages. The process of becoming a disciple, and then a disciple-maker, is how we make being "like Jesus" or "Christ-like" (aka: Christian) second nature! (Again, you cannot and will not be or produce something you are not!) Remember the definition of "second nature" is "an acquired, deeply ingrained habit or skill." Just as brushing your teeth has become second nature, so can being a disciple-maker!

Jesus shared a parable in the Sermon on the Mount: "A blind man cannot guide a blind man, can he? Will they not both fall into a pit? A disciple is not above his teacher; but everyone, after he has been fully trained, will be like his teacher."[2] I love what Jesus expresses in this passage: (1) If you're following someone who doesn't know what they're doing, all you've got waiting for you is a pit; (2) This isn't about a hierarchical system, but

2 - Lk. 6:39-40

an impartation; (3) If you're in His kingdom, He wants *everyone* fully trained to become like Him. Notice I didn't say become an apostle, prophet, evangelist, pastor, or teacher; although that could be your eventual destiny if He deems it so. Jesus encapsulated all five of those offices, but He came without a religious or positional title. Instead, He came as a mere carpenter.

In His book *Approaching the Heart of Prophecy*, Graham Cooke posed the questions, "What if the problems in the world are not lawlessness and crime; not poverty and sickness; not greed and selfishness; not drugs or terrorism; not abortion or immorality? What if the biggest problem in the earth is simply the lack of goodness?"[x] He then addressed his questions by saying, "The ambassadors of Christ are spewing out judgment in the name of righteous indignation and the world is going to hell because we have misunderstood the glory of God. When Moses asked to see the glory of God, the Father showed him His goodness whilst proclaiming His compassion."[xi]

The world wants to know what God is like. Jesus came to put a face on God, and the church is present to put a face on Christ Jesus: "He who has seen Me, has seen the Father."[3] Graham was essentially saying that we spend way too much time cutting off the "dandelion heads," the symptoms of sin, instead of getting to the root of the sin problem. As ambassadors of Christ, we should focus on the goodness and glory of God. Through discipleship, we can impart this goodness and glory as it emanates from our intimate relationship that we build with the Lord.

3 - Jn. 14:9b (NASB)

My friend, Todd Durkin, is one of the nation's top physical fitness trainers. A few years back, he participated in a fitness competition reality television show on NBC called *Strong*. As you may remember from his foreword here, one of his mantras is "10 In-10 Out!" In other words, what you put in is exactly what you get out! But, in God's kingdom, if you put in ten, you could get back a hundredfold because of His principle of sowing and reaping![4]

I wonder what would happen if we were to change our focus from the notion of simply getting people *saved* to the notion of getting people *saved and discipled in order to display His goodness*. I wonder if we might start to see some legitimate exponential growth happen here in America and of course across the world. I'm not presenting these questions this way to denigrate the ambassadors of Christ in America or any other place for that matter, but rather to express my frustration produced from experiential knowledge, having been involved with three different church movements and churches growing through transfer growth (moving from one church to another church); but as far as salvific growth (adding by new salvations) is concerned, our numbers are down in America. This is why a dear friend, Dr. Rice Broocks, who wrote the *God's Not Dead* book series, is bent on spearheading an evangelistic movement throughout the world. I'm convinced that if you take an evangelistic movement coupled with a legitimate black belt-discipleship movement and unleash it on the world, we might just see the fulfillment of what Graham Cooke said the world wanted to see—what God is truly like.

4 - Mk. 4:3-8

Second Nature

We need a Jesus-type of personal and corporate refocusing. A prophecy about Jesus, the ideal disciple, says, "For the Lord God helps Me, therefore, I am not disgraced; Therefore, I have set my face like flint, and I know that I will not be ashamed."[5] And we know from the Bible that there was nothing that could deter Jesus from His purpose nor the pleasing of His Father. "And He who sent Me is with Me; He has not left Me alone, for I always do the things that are pleasing to Him!"[6]

It's no secret that our lives are too busy and some serious pruning needs to take place. Sometimes pastors think we have to get the congregation involved in multiple activities to keep their attention and their tithes. Instead, we should be helping them with the reprioritization of their spiritual life by helping them get focused on the task that Jesus gave us. Truth be told, people only have so many activity slots in their lives. And if they overextend, they eventually burn out and, sadly, jettison church activities first. The apostle Paul was good at avoiding the burnout phase. He said, "For I determined to know nothing among you except Jesus Christ, and Him crucified."[7]

Jesus was crucified to do away with sin, to bring us into His family, and to make us His disciples, so we could, in turn, go do the same to the world. He was first focused on His Father, and then on people! Paul told his disciple Timothy, "Suffer hardship with me, as a good soldier of Christ Jesus. No soldier in active service entangles himself in the affairs of everyday life, so that he may please the one who enlisted him as a soldier."[8] These are the words of

5 - Isa. 50:7

6 - Jn. 8:29

7 - 1 Cor. 2:2

8 - 2 Tim. 2:3-4

life according to Jesus! It's a simple matter of prioritizing our lives correctly.

Jesus began this thing with making disciples, and He wants to finish it by returning to a plethora of black belt disciple-makers imparting the nature of a disciple-maker. He is the original black belt disciple-maker. And if we want to become like Him, according to His will, then we, too, will become black belt disciple-makers. I see such tenacity and focus by people in other areas of life, be it starting a business, getting their bodies into shape, reaching their vocational goals, etc. But when it comes to the quality of our spiritual life, it's the proverbial app on the phone; we just open up the app to some God when we need help and close the app when we're finished.

I believe we should have the same type of resolve for that which Jesus has given us to do that He had for that which the Father had given Him to do: "When the days drew near for him to be taken up, he set his face to Jerusalem."[9] The phrase "set his face" is a Hebrew idiom meaning, *he was determined.*[xii] Jesus was determined to be a disciple of the Father.[10] Jesus was determined to give the best example of what that looked like and put it on display to be the antithesis of what the religious sect had put out there as the example.[11] Jesus was determined to go to the cross so that we could become His family members and disciple-makers while here on Earth. Is that same kind of determination to be Jesus' version of disciple-makers normally seen throughout our congregations?

As human beings, we are so used to seeing things

9 - Lk. 9:51 (ESV)
10 - Isa. 50:5
11 - Jn. 5:19

done better, faster, or more efficiently because of technology. But when it comes to people, it's important to remember that they are not *things* that are to be done more efficiently as if they were tasks or tools. People are created in the image of the Heavenly Father, which ascribes instant value. People can feel when they are being used or judged as opposed to being valued or encouraged.

When it comes to God, we need to get back to the ancient paths. As the Word reveals, "Thus says the Lord, 'Stand by the ways and see and ask for the ancient paths, where the good way is, and walk in it; and you will find rest for your souls.' But they said, 'We will not walk in it.' And I set watchmen over you, saying, 'Listen to the sound of the trumpet!' But they said, 'We will not listen.'"[12]

I think it's pretty obvious that here in America we are not walking in the "ancient paths" by making disciples the way Jesus made disciples. And I'm not quite sure that the watchmen, the pastors, are truly blowing the spiritual trumpets to get people back to these ancient paths.

Throughout this book we looked at stages of growth disciples must go through, checkpoints for them to gauge their progress. We talked about how the process should involve a relationship rather than merely the dissemination of information. We looked at the heart of ancient discipleship and held it up against today's version of discipleship in America. Here's a provocative saying that some have attributed to Mahatma Gandhi: "I like your Christ. I do not like your Christians. Your Christians are so unlike Christ."

12 - Jer. 6:16-17 (NASB)

I question whether Gandhi really liked our Christ or not. Like many people in the world, I believe Gandhi had his own made-up version of Jesus to suit his musings and to soothe his conscience as well. But I understand the sentiment, to a certain extent, because Jesus never called us to be Christians first, but to become disciples in order to become like Him—ergo, truly Christians! A friend of mine once made this statement: "People don't reject Jesus; they reject man's version of Jesus." Well, I think the more we truly become like Him through discipleship, the less the world will be deceived into thinking they have an excuse not to follow Him.

Here are three things that will never change in the kingdom of God: (1) All that is good and kingdom-oriented is founded on the love and lordship of Jesus Christ. (2) It always comes back to discipleship. And (3) everything rests on your perspective, so you had better get God's perspective! This whole time I've been trying to drive home the vision of God for our lives—to accurately represent Him here on Earth. Our biggest problem is that we lose sight of this vision. Oswald Chambers said this:

> *If we lose the vision, we alone are responsible, and the way we lose the vision is by spiritual leakage. If we do not run our belief about God into practical issues, it is all up with the vision God has given. The only way to be obedient to the heavenly vision is to give our utmost for God's highest, and this can only be done by continually and resolutely recalling the vision.*[xiii]

Jesus gave a vision of what discipleship looks like, and He started with a big if—"If any man will come after Me..."[13]

That *if* is a whole-hearted appeal from the Lord for you to take hold of the potential birthed inside of you by receiving the salvation He purchased on your behalf upon the cross. It's much like what coaches see in someone who has raw talent. They see the potential, the possibilities, as opposed to just the current production. They desire to make every effort to bring the *possible* into a state of *reality*. The first step a coach takes is to try to impress upon the athlete the importance, the dire need, to master the essentials that will bring about that reality and get rid of the non-essentials with extreme prejudice.

The spiritual graveyard parallels the natural graveyard in the amount of untapped potential that has been wasted and buried. If you have received Christ as Lord, will you allow yourself to become a spiritual casualty, or will you become a disciple as Jesus intended? The first essential condition required is to *deny yourself*.

I believe you can become a casualty in regards to God's ultimate purpose for your life, though not in regards to your position in Him. This happens when you don't fulfill your full potential, even though you desire to. Leonardo Da Vinci had this to say, "Knowing is not enough, you must apply; being is not enough, you must do." Sounds like Da Vinci stole that from the lil' green prophet, Yoda, from Star Wars who said, "Do or do not, there is no try." Oswald Chambers shared his musings about discipleship as well: "*Our Lord never lays down*

13 - Lk. 9:23 (KJV)

the conditions of discipleship as the conditions of salvation. We are condemned to salvation through the Cross of Jesus Christ. Discipleship has an option with it—'IF any man...'"[xiv] So I believe the *casualty or not* part is up to you and me, depending on how we respond to that big "*If*."

    Discipleship is not about transmitting some information about God; it's about transferring the life of Christ. To be a discipler, you must first be a disciple. Jesus is most definitely the greatest black belt disciple-maker of all time and He wants you to join Him. Jesus, like any great sensei, has left that decision in your hands. But remember, you cannot and will not *ever* be or produce something you are not! Now, are you ready to get your black belt? I'm not sure where you were in your discipleship journey before you picked up this book. And I'm not sure where you are now after having read it. But, if you're stepping into the discipleship dojo, that's great! If you're already in, even better! Either way, let's do this--that black belt is ready to be had! As Sir Anthony Hopkins told Antonio Bandaras in the movie *The Mask of Zorro*, "When the pupil is ready, the master will appear!"

Cool Down Devotional Stretches:

One thing is for sure--what you do is what you become! I became a better football player and basketball player the more I practiced and the more I played. My Heavenly Father gifted me with the ability to sing, but I became a better singer when I acquired a vocal teacher later in life and truly learned how to use my instrument. And what I found to be unequivocally undeniable in my life is that I became a better disciple of Jesus when I started discipling others! People are generally afraid to tell someone to follow them, imitate them, unless they are confident, that they have the "goods." Unless they know that what they want to give to you is second nature to them. I am over that hurdle. I have no problem at all humbly telling someone to "Imitate me as I imitate Christ!"[14] And you won't either! See, if you study that scripture intently, you will discover that Jesus is the benchmark in it—not you or me! As long as you keep your eyes on Jesus just like He kept His eyes on His Father in heaven, you will be covered by His grace and enabled to do all that He has called you to!

Whelp, here we are, time for a respite. Time to strip down to your spiritual "birthday suit" and take a hard look at who you are in Christ. Have you been the kind of Christian who tells themselves that making disciples is more about an extroverted versus an introverted personality rather than an acquired skill that becomes a habitual lifestyle? Do you see anyone in your sphere of influence that has disciples, that are making disciples, that are making disciples? You can pray for God to bring someone into your life to be just that kind of mentor and disciple-maker. Please also connect with me through a social media platform—I have a discipleship dojo you can step into!

14 - 1 Cor. 11:1 (ESV)

Acknowledgements

To those who played a role early in the formational journey of me becoming, not only a disciple but a disciple-maker, I will forever be indebted...you know who you are. To Sam and Erin Hancock, what was such a small thing to you, was an incredibly huge thing for me; thank you from the very depths of my heart! To my mother Erma Jean Mingo (aka: Mama Mingo) who taught me to love God more than anyone else in my life (even her), I want to thank you for the way you have loved me. You have been the biggest and greatest ministry partner that my Lion Pride and I could have ever had—your crown in heaven is going to be too heavy to wear, so just cast it down and worship Him! To my five lioness cubs, Noelle, Moriah, Sophia, Morgan, and Ginger, you obviously have no other choice but to be disciples and make disciples since it is all you have ever heard me talk about since your birth. There is no doubt, by the grace of God, you are Mommy and Daddy's greatest accomplishments in life! Michelle, in December of 2000 I gave you a figurine of Simba with Nala's head nuzzled in Simba's neck; you have always made me feel kingly. God has blessed me with you as my ride-or-die where failure is just simply not an option...I love you to LIFE!!!

Suggested Reading

The Purple Book:
Biblical Foundations For Building Strong Disciples
by: Rice Brooks and Steve Murrell

Wikichurch:
Making Discipleship Engaging, Empowering, & Viral
by: Steve Murrell

The Multiplication Challenge:
A Strategy to Solve Your Leadership Shortage
by: Steve Murrell & William Murrell

Notes

i - Scriven, Joseph, "What a Friend We Have in Jesus," *https://www.hymnal.net/en/hymn/h/789.*

ii - Leonard, George, *Mastery: The Keys To Successful And Long-Term Fulfillment* (New York: Penguin Books USA Inc., 1992), p. 4.

iii - Easton, Matthew George, ed. (1897), *Illustrated Bible Dictionary* (also known as *Easton's Bible Dictionary, 3rd Edition)* (London: T. Nelson & Sons), "government."

iv - Barna Group, Continental U.S. Study (2018).

v - Chambers, Oswald, *My Utmost For His Highest* (Michigan: Barbour Publishing Inc., 1935), October 27th.

vi - Brannan, Rick, Lexham *Analytical Lexicon to the Greek New Testament*, 13.32, 36.19. 37.122, Logos Bible software, 2008.

vii - Hawkins, Dr. O.S., "Go the Second Mile," (excerpt from *The Joshua Code* by O.S. Hawkins, published by Thomas Nelson, quoted on http://faithgateway.com).

viii - Edwards, Jonathan, 1703-1758. "Sinners in the Hands of an Angry God." (A Sermon, Preached at Enfield, Connecticut, July 8, 1741).

ix - Maxwell, John C., *The 5 Levels of Leadership* (New York: Center Street Hachette Book Group, 2011), 181-182.

x - Cooke, Graham, *Approaching the Heart of Prophecy* (CA: Brilliant Book House, LLC, 2006), 13.

xi - Ibid., v.

xii - Benner, Jeff A., "Ancient Hebrew Idioms," https://www.ancient-hebrew.org/language/ancient-hebrew-idioms.htm, 11/28/2020.

xiii - Chambers, *Utmost*, March 11th.

xiv - Chambers, *Utmost*, February 2nd.

Available

on Kindle, Google Play, Nook, and iBooks.

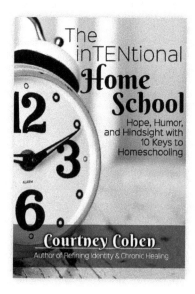

Available

in print and eBook from

NOW FOUND
P U B L I S H I N G

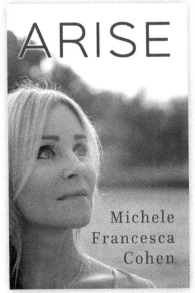
ARISE

Michele
Francesca
Cohen

FOREWORD BY JAN GREENWOOD
AUTHOR OF *WOMEN AT WAR*

REFINING
IDENTITY

I Am *Who* I AM *Says* I Am

COURTNEY COHEN

EDENSONG

REVELATIONS OF IDENTITY

Michele Francesca Cohen

Chronic
Healing

Courtney Cohen

FOREWORD BY MONDOE DAVIS
FORMER NFL LINE BACKER

Hope and
Healing
for Body, Soul,
& Spirit

Coming Soon

from

Loved As You Are: A Family Journey of Adoption
provides hope and love to overcome the stuggles and hardships
children adopted through foster care may experience along the
way.

Also Available

in print from

God knew us before time existed....
Where Your Beginning Began: A Family Journey of Adoption
helps ensure that children adopted through private adoption
know who and whose they are.

Now Available
in print and eBook from

NOW FOUND
PUBLISHING

What **LIES** Beneath
from **LIES** to Love

FOREWORD BY:
COURTNEY COHEN
The Sacred Shadow

STEVEN
COHEN

COURTNEY COHEN
AUTHOR OF *REFINING IDENTITY* & *CHRONIC HEALING*

THE
SACRED SHADOW
ENTER INTO THE DAILY MYSTERY OF GOD'S KINGDOM
FOREWORD BY: CHRISTINE D'CLARIO

CDs Available

at GinoMingo.com

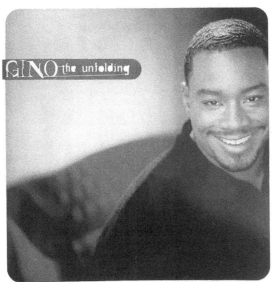

About Gino

Pastor, singer/songwriter, and author of *Black Belt Discipleship*, Gino Mingo helps people pursue Jesus through a lifestyle of radical, transformational discipleship. As a former member of both the NFL and CFL, Gino learned early on the importance of dedication and sacrifice, but that was nothing compared to the adventure he found through understanding the call of Christ.

Gino and his wife, Michelle, were both brought up in church, but came to a transformational faith in Jesus in their twenties. They became close friends working together in campus ministry, were married, and now live in San Diego with their five daughters (yes — five daughters!) where they lead **ROAR Ministries**.

Gino's ministry philosophy is profoundly simple: love God, love people, and make disciples. Stay in touch with Gino at **GinoMingo.com**.

Live, Create & Share Your Story

Your story is powerful. Do you have a message you long to share with others, but aren't sure how to begin? Do you want to see lives changed, but writing isn't your strong suit? Do you long to see your heart's message in print, but are overwhelmed with the idea of becoming published? If so, we would be honored to serve and assist you.

At **Now Found Publishing**, we walk alongside authors through every step of the writing and publishing process. We provide services including proofreading, all levels of editing, coaching, cover design, and formatting while maintaining the heart of your message and your individual voice. Contact us at: **authors@nowfoundpublishing.com** to live, create, and share your story.

For information on **Now Found Publishing** and our inspirational and life-changing resources, visit **NowFoundPublishing.com**.